Praise for

I'LL BE HOME

"Jim McGrath was a great American voice, a no-nonsense journalist who wrote eloquently about intolerance, injustice, poverty, and corruption. He wasn't afraid to tell the truth, and he did so masterfully. His work is inspiring, witty, profound, and kindhearted. No wonder so many held him in high esteem—even those he skewered."
— Sam Roe, *Chicago Tribune*

"For me, Albany has always been home, and it was the great honor and privilege of my life to have been its mayor for twenty years. For Jim, Albany, became his adopted home, a place he loved and cared for as passionately as I did and that mutual love for this place was the bond we shared. Even when we disagreed, we respected each other's commitment to our community and to its residents who relied on us in different, but equally important ways. And whether it was across the table at an editorial board meeting, or sharing a beverage at McGeary's, Jim was never hesitant to speak truth to power. His writings, many of which I took issue with, always reflected his commitment to honesty, accuracy, and fairness. That commitment made Albany a better city and without question it made me a better mayor. This book bears witness to Jim's legacy and to the impact he had on our community and on so many lives. It also serves as a testament to the vital role a great journalist plays in the vibrancy of our democratic process. The lessons to be learned here could not come at a better time. For all that we are in his debt."
— Jerry Jennings, Mayor of Albany, 1994–2013

"Jim's arguments were thoughtful and his writing was elegant. But what stands out most in this collection are his passion and his humanity. His passion for journalism. His passion for fairness. His passion for truth. He railed against injustice. He scoffed at heavy-handed politics. He spoke out on behalf of those who couldn't speak for themselves. Even in print, you could see his arms waving in outrage as he called upon society to rectify another of its shortcomings."
— Benjamin Weller, *Newsday*

I'll Be Home

Jim on Duck Harbor Beach in Wellfleet, Massachusetts, on the far end of Cape Cod, September 2001. Jim and Darryl divided their honeymoon into two parts: Chicago in June 2001, and the Outer Cape in September 2001. Reading, mentally editing, and critiquing the local newspapers, no matter where he was, came naturally to Jim. Here, he is almost certainly studying the *Cape Cod Times* or the *Boston Globe*. Photograph by Darryl McGrath.

I'll Be Home

◆

THE WRITINGS OF
JIM McGRATH

Edited by

Darryl McGrath *and* Howard Healy

excelsior editions
AN IMPRINT OF STATE UNIVERSITY OF NEW YORK PRESS

Published by
STATE UNIVERSITY OF NEW YORK PRESS, ALBANY

© 2019 State University of New York

EXCELSIOR EDITIONS IS AN IMPRINT OF STATE UNIVERSITY OF NEW YORK PRESS

For information, contact State University of New York Press, Albany, NY
www.sunypress.edu

Library of Congress Cataloging-in-Publication Data

Names: McGrath, Jim, 1957–2013, author. | McGrath, Darryl, 1957– editor. |
    Healy, Howard, 1941– editor.
Title: I'll be home : the writings of Jim McGrath / edited by Darryl McGrath and
    Howard Healy.
Description: Albany : State University of New York, [2019] | Series: Excelsior editions
Identifiers: LCCN 2018027992 | ISBN 9781438474229 (paperback : alk. paper) |
    ISBN 9781438474243 (e-book)
Subjects: LCSH: McGrath, Jim, 1957–2013. | Journalists—New York (State)—
    Albany—Biography.
Classification: LCC PN4874.M3725 A25 2019 | DDC 070.92 [B] —dc23
LC record available at https://lccn.loc.gov/2018027992

10   9   8   7   6   5   4   3   2   1

His words conveyed beauty, passion, indignation, empathy, outrage, humor, and, ultimately, love.

—Darryl McGrath,
Albany author and journalist

In print he was thoughtful, generous, sympathetic, never cynical, and always laced with the wry wit he seemed to come by naturally.

—Fred LeBrun,
metro columnist and former reporter and
editor for the *Albany Times Union*

. . . many professional writers familiar with his work, myself included, often found themselves reading McGrath and muttering privately, "I wish I had written that."

—Dan Lynch,
former managing editor and
columnist for the *Albany Times Union*

He could comment on almost any topic with clarity, concision, and lasting persuasiveness . . .

—Robert Whitcomb,
former editorial-page editor of the *Providence Journal*

Contents

Foreword

When the Newspaper Needed to Speak from Its Soul

Rex Smith

It is almost shocking to read Jim McGrath's words now, these few years after he was prematurely silenced—shocking because it reminds us of how swiftly time passes and life changes, and yet how close we remain to a disappearing world he chronicled with such exquisite candor.

For in reading these essays, we open a window into our recent past, enabling us to witness again the passion that fueled civic dialogue on issues now already slipping into oblivion, or, in some cases, transformed into today's real-life conflicts. If the quick passage of time exposed by these transitory battles is unsettling, it's also clarifying, for we see how much of our life today is built, piece by piece, on day-by-day decisions made years before. How fortunate the community was that for a while it had Jim McGrath analyzing those daily decisions.

Jim wrote what he thought every day, and it was quickly published for tens of thousands of people to consider. This thought-to-page daily exercise was a requirement of his job during his years as the *Times Union*'s chief editorial writer. It is a discipline that makes it almost impossible for a writer to conceal his or her innermost self, for a character is exposed in such small increments. On display in this volume, then, are essays that you may consider the expositions of Jim's heart—a big heart, surely, though one sadly unable to accommodate the years its host should have been granted on this earth.

Of course, the editorial writing process involves an ensemble, as Jim always pointed out. Typically, before sitting down to write, Jim would huddle with a handful of other editors and haggle over the meaning of an event or what we might be able to conclude from what had been reported that day. He was not at all reluctant to attempt to steer the conversation to match his personal viewpoint, even in a group of similarly strong-willed journalists.

Nobody who sat in that room weekday mornings with Jim will ever forget it. His voice booming, arms flailing, he would sometimes launch into a sentence before having figured out entirely where he intended to end it, a roiling wave of opinion that finally washed over us complete, leaving us simply nodding. "Yeah, do that, Jim," one would say. Then he would go off to cast his concepts into words, coming up with the crafted essay a few hours later, ready to be published in the morning newspaper—at which point the process would begin again.

You will be struck as you read this book, I suspect, by the passion that the writer brings to his arguments. This won't surprise anybody who knew Jim—a big, sometimes blustery Irishman—but what also comes through is a meticulousness in the writing that is pure McGrath. His mastery of the writing craft led to Jim being called upon whenever the newspaper needed to speak from its soul, as on the anniversary of the 9/11 attacks. In one piece after another here, you will see an old-fashioned elegance in Jim's prose that speaks of his reverence for the language and his understanding of the place where his writing was being published.

Albany wasn't Jim's home, after all, until he adopted it as that—and then he embraced it as a grateful adoptive parent would a child. In this 300-year-old American city, he found echoes of both the Boston of his childhood and the Chicago he came to know as a young man. It's not an exaggeration to say that Jim loved the petty corruption of Albany, the remaining traces of its decades-long machine rule, the contemporary characters who in his imagination could have been fodder for a new generation's William Kennedy, the great novelist (and *Times Union* alumnus) who adapted Albany history to the discipline of fiction. Kennedy's work reflects his love for the place, Albany; McGrath's work, even in its sometimes scolding or saddened voice, no less does the same. If he hadn't written with love, Jim McGrath wouldn't have won the authentic reflection of love from his readers.

But he did. Day after day, Jim McGrath's work brought the *Times Union* closer to its readers, sometimes by exhorting them, sometimes by chastising them, sometimes by comforting them. This volume also includes unpublished material and articles unseen by most of his Albany-area readers, and in these are gems, too. In all, this work is a remarkable reflection on a time so recently here, yet now so quickly gone. As was Jim McGrath. We miss him still, but we are left, fortunately, with these words of his. And so we treasure them.

Rex Smith is editor of the *Times Union*.

Introduction

HOWARD HEALY

This book is a tribute, a testament, and a portrait.

It is a tribute to Jim McGrath, a valued colleague of mine for more than a decade at the *Times Union*. It is also a testament to Jim's stature as a journalist and writer, as can been seen in the articles, editorials, commentary, and recollections that are collected here. And it is a portrait because, after you finish reading this book, you will have gotten to know Jim in all his dimensions—as a seeker of justice, as a voice for the marginalized, as a conscience for a community that often tried to deny its failings. It also shows Jim's other side—his generosity of spirit, his loyalty to friends, his unwavering allegiance to the Red Sox, his memories of growing up in Boston, his love of Albany, even his nostalgic, almost sentimental, attachment to a pay telephone booth that stood lonely and unused in the age of the smartphone. And much more.

More than anything, though, this book is a work of love. It was inspired by Jim's loving wife, Darryl, who saw it through from concept to the final printed volume. It was her hard work and steadfast loyalty to the memory of her husband that made possible the book you are now holding in your hands. I was privileged to work with Darryl as a coeditor of what we informally called "the Jim book." I contributed my memories of working with Jim, some of which are included elsewhere in this volume. I also offered my advice when warranted, but mostly I just stood by, in awe of Darryl's devotion.

Together we selected what we considered to be the best examples of Jim's writing. It was no easy task as Jim wrote more than 3,000 editorials, features, opinion pieces, and essays during his nearly 40 years in journalism. A few of the pieces that made our cut have never before been published, but we thought they deserved to be, and so they are in this book. And one piece included here Jim did not write at all. It is a transcript of a radio interview he did the day Governor Spitzer resigned, and it is included because you can hear how Jim's mind framed an editorial by the way he spoke. It's also vintage Jim, for its enthusiastic tone and its subtly sardonic wit.

We decided to catalog the 62 pieces we selected under six categories: "Albany," "Politics," "Social Justice," "Journalism," "Sports," and a sixth category called "I'll Be Home." That last section contains more personal writings, including a fellowship application essay that sketched out the early plans for a memoir Jim had hoped to write, and from which the title of this book is taken. If you knew Jim McGrath, or just admired his writing from afar, this book's long roster of names and places, issues and events, will resonate. But if you're not familiar with Jim's work, we suggest you begin with the "I'll Be Home" section, which contains some of Jim's longer works on topics that touch all our lives—family struggles, small triumphs, sudden joys and lingering disappointments, heartache, life and death. Jim wrote about them all.

Our contributors wrote several of the introductions to various sections, as well as the foreword to the book, a very fitting appreciation of Jim and an intimately knowledgeable description of the Albany that Jim knew so well and loved so much.

The opening epigraphs are excerpts from the essays of some of those contributors. Their words speak for themselves. But Jim's words make up most of this book. They speak for themselves, too, Jim's words, their power unbroken.

Howard Healy was the editorial page editor at the *Albany Times Union* from 1988 to 2008.

ALBANY

When Jim moved to Albany from Florida, in 1985, he got a second-floor apartment in a house on Hudson Avenue, on the block between Albany's Lark Street and Washington Park. He loved the location so much that he vowed he would never live anywhere in Albany farther than an easy walk from Lark Street. The house that he bought with Darryl in 2004 on Irving Street in Albany's Hudson/Park neighborhood was five minutes from Lark Street and Jim's favorite hangout, the Lark Tavern, on Madison Avenue, just around the corner from Lark. Here, in an undated photo, he enjoys the Albany tradition of sitting on the front stoop to take in the scene from the Irving Street house. Photograph by Darryl McGrath.

Introduction

The City That Jim Embraced

HOWARD HEALY

The title of this book—*I'll Be Home*—doesn't mention where home is. It doesn't have to. Anyone who knew Jim McGrath, either as a friend, neighbor, or colleague, or just a stranger he had met the day before, knew that Jim's home was Albany. It didn't matter that he was born in Boston, or that he went to college outside Chicago, or that he worked at a string of newspapers in the Midwest and South before arriving here. What mattered was that Jim adopted Albany as his true home more than any place else—and the city embraced him as much as he embraced it.

When Jim arrived in Albany, his previous two newspaper jobs had been at the *Hartford Courant* and the *Sun-Tattler*, in Hollywood, Florida, and he was still in search of a permanent home. He knew he never wanted to return to Florida, where the *Sun-Tattler* had served snowbird communities, where every face was white and every neighborhood indistinguishable from the other. Jim wanted to remain in the Northeast, but Hartford wasn't the right fit. Albany, on the other hand, was the perfect fit. Here was a city with a deep history, historic districts in the shadow of modern architecture, diverse neighborhoods, working-class hangouts, and colorful, often quirky characters. No question that Albany reminded Jim of Boston, but his attraction to Albany was not based on memories of his urban roots. It was a genuine connection—as strong a bond as if he had been born here.

Jim was no dreamer, though. As much as he loved Albany, he knew it suffered the same ills as any Rust Belt city upstate—an aging infrastructure, white flight, poverty, homelessness, crime, declining neighborhoods, underperforming schools and vicious school board politics, and racial tensions, especially between police and minority communities. Rather than flee from Albany's failings by settling in the suburbs (imagine Jim living in Clifton Park—impossible!), Jim wrote forceful editorials calling for change and supporting worthy reforms. Sometimes he wrote from personal experience. Take declining neighborhoods as one example. He once lived on Morris Street, where one night he had to fight off an intruder, and where he witnessed firsthand the plague of drugs and the cynicism of bad landlords.

For all of that, Jim loved living downtown and being close to Washington Park, even though he was once mugged there. His first apartment was a short walk to the park, on Hudson Avenue, adjacent to the former Planned Parenthood building parking lot, and he would sit out on the second-floor balcony sipping his coffee and reading the newspaper he had helped put out the night before. He loved that ritual, and he loved neighborhood pubs like the Lark Tavern (his second home when he first arrived here) and later McGeary's. He knew where every mom-and-pop diner and late-night eatery was, and all the characters who populated them.

Of course, there was the matter of Albany politics. What would Albany be without politics? But this section is about more than politics alone. It's about Albany as a city, its people, its places, its struggles, its charm. In other words, it's about home—Jim's home. Even at that, though, two points need to be made.

One is Jim's generosity, which was never more on display than around the holidays. As Jim's dear wife Darryl tells it, Jim couldn't bear the thought that someone he knew, or had just met, might be alone when others were gathered in celebration. So the guest list at the McGrath household would grow—and grow, and grow—as a holiday approached. On at least one occasion, an extension had to be added to the dining room table.

The second point is about "Chicago," that paean to the city of big shoulders by Carl Sandburg. It was Jim's favorite poem, no doubt because it captured the essence of a city he knew well from his college days. But Jim's Albany has to be described differently, much differently. As long as he was writing watchdog editorials, and as long as his door was open to those in need of a warm welcome, Albany—Jim's Albany—could only be described thusly: city with a strong conscience—and an outsize heart.

Howard Healy had a career in newspapers that spanned 45 years, working for publications as varied as the *Troy Record*, the Louisville *Courier-Journal*, the *Wall Street Journal*, the *Knickerbocker News*, and the Albany *Times Union*, where he served as editorial page editor from 1988 to 2008. He now works for the New York State Bar Association.

The Race Is On in Albany

Times Union editorial, January 16, 1997

The suspense, such as it ever was, over whether state assemblyman John J. McEneny would run for mayor is past. It really isn't much of a surprise that he's in the race, either. The real question now is this: What kind of campaign can Albany expect?

Already, Mayor Jennings is annoyed by the prospect of a Democratic primary, particularly for the very office he already holds. In Albany, though, the Democratic primary will be the mayoral election, this year and, most likely, for more than a few years to come. Mayor Jennings knows that as well as Mr. McEneny does. If the mayor tries to overlook that, the election results from four years ago should be enough to remind him—his successful but bruising primary against Harold Joyce and then the general election against Republican Phil Sprio that was barely a contest at all.

The mayor has also made note of the fact that the 1993 primary wasn't a challenge to an incumbent. But that's not the issue. At least it shouldn't be. A primary campaign instead offers Albany, to its enrolled Democrats and everyone else, the chance for an open and serious debate about the city's future.

Mr. McEneny says the city is in decline, that the middle class is leaving, that the schools need to be better, and that property values are falling. Mayor Jennings, of course, will challenge such claims. He'll point to his record as mayor, and it certainly is one that he should defend, not as a relentless volley of campaign charges and countercharges but as a thoughtful argument about what's best for the city.

Mr. McEneny and Mayor Jennings should talk about strengthening the city's tax base—there should have been a reassessment long ago—and finding a way for City Hall to assert a positive and measurable influence on public education even as it honors the autonomy of the school district. A race between two natives of Albany who have spent their lives in the public sector actually could be an uplifting one. It certainly does not have to be a repeat of the often petty, and even ugly, 1993 primary.

Let's have a campaign rich in ideas, but not one where big money wins out. The mayor spent $400,000 on the primary against Mr. Joyce. The last big election in Albany, the Neil Breslin–Michael Hoblock state Senate race in November, cost more than $1 million. There's no reason for that, not in a city the size of Albany. This time, though, Mr. McEneny already is talking about keeping campaign contributions to the $500 range.

And let's have a campaign run by people from Albany. It's discouraging, frankly, to learn that the mayor is talking about bringing in a hired gun from New York City who last worked on President Clinton's reelection campaign. Aside from, perhaps, Mr. McEneny, who better knows how to run for office around here than the mayor himself?

The race is on. We're looking forward to it, and we hope the city benefits from it.

A Sad Note on Lark Street

Times Union editorial, February 19, 1997

Sad as it was, the news broke in the right place, right here in the paper. Fowler's, the newsstand and card store on Lark Street in Albany, is closing on Monday. It's a shame to see part of any family business go under, but this one hits close to home.

First off, we'll remember it as a newsstand. The greeting cards and the gifts were nice, we suppose, and they sold candy and that sort of thing, but we went there for newspapers and magazines. No sooner would the door open than Frank, behind the counter, would be pointing out that the new issue of the *Nation* was in and that Christopher Hitchens or Alexander Cockburn had a good piece. Oh, and there was a good piece in the *New Yorker* this week, and, hey, what about the latest bombshell in the New York City tabloids?

Fowler's was the sort of place where they didn't complain when you browsed through the expensive, high-brow foreign policy magazines that you wouldn't buy, but they'd let you know if the cops were outside ticketing cars. It was the sort of place where Mrs. Fowler, the boss, would point out errors in our own paper, in a pleasant but direct way that probably wasn't much different from how she did it when she taught English down the street at Hackett. It was, especially, the sort of place that built up loyal—fondly loyal—customers over the years.

Its closing points out how Lark Street is changing. Finally, an Italian restaurant and market is coming to the old Lemme's Market, at the corner of State Street, which has been a big wooden nothing for a few years now. At the same intersection, where the State Street Pub used to be, it has been the same story. Oh, and the Larkin, the restaurant across the street from Fowler's, is closed, at least for now.

Elsewhere, though, and especially heading down the street toward Madison Avenue, the pulse of a rather eclectic street in a not-too-big city throbs as it always did. There's coffee, good coffee, and something stronger, too, to be had on just about every block. There's still a good mix of places to get something to eat. The Waldorf tuxedo place in that neat brownstone at the corner of Lancaster is a landmark on the street, and, hey, there just aren't too many places in town where you can get a tattoo.

Lark Street will endure. We'll bet on that, with our heads and our hearts.

It's just that it won't be quite, well, the same.

Slayings Tarnish Soil of Albany's Great Park

Times Union, bylined opinion piece, December 26, 1997

The nightly holiday lights display in Albany's Washington Park had been over for just a few hours when two teenagers were confronted by robbers, forced to their knees, and shot and killed. The predawn gunshots startled the neighborhood. By sunrise, the southeast corner of the park was a display of its own, a crime scene in full view of the morning commuters. If ever there was a time for a city to take stock of itself, it was right then, Friday, December 19, 1997.

Larry Omar Miller, 18, and Lamel Wells Robinson, 17, are the second and third people found dead in the park in just four months. The slayings come, too, not long after the city had a debate of sorts about crime during the mayoral campaign. Mayor Jerry Jennings had been saying, in essence, that he'd walk anywhere in Albany, any time. His unsuccessful opponent, state Assemblyman Jack McEneny, ridiculed the mayor for making such an assertion. For that, he was roundly criticized in some quarters for being irresponsible.

But now two kids are dead because they did walk in Albany, through Washington Park at the oddest of hours. Perhaps it's time to talk and to talk more reasonably about crime in Albany.

The public, and the press as well, has some oddly discriminating interests when it comes to crime. Often they rise to utter fascination. When a deeply disturbed gunman takes a classroom hostage and seriously wounds a student at the University at Albany, the result is a public fixation and huge headlines. An innocent young girl rushes to open what appears to be a holiday package in her family's home in a Clifton Park subdivision, and there's an appetite for as many details as possible that extends well beyond the Capital Region. But the trauma in the classroom three years ago did nothing to diminish the value of a UAlbany education. Clifton Park is no less a desirable place to live because a package exploded on someone's dining room table last Christmas Eve.

In Albany, in and around Washington Park, that luxury of irrelevance simply isn't there. To read about the senseless slayings of Larry Omar Miller and Lamel Wells Robinson just might be what it takes to turn to the classifieds and see what's for rent or for sale uptown, or across the river or out in the suburbs.

You'll never quite find the soul and pulse of Albany in those buildings downtown, grand as they are, where laws are made, justice is carried out, and political plots are hatched. But you very well might find it in Washington Park. In the spring, tens upon thousands of people come to admire the tulips and free themselves, finally, from an upstate winter. In the summer, the music onstage at the Lakehouse can be nothing short of spectacular. Time was when the brilliance of Shakespeare came alive on a stage along the parade grounds. Last fall at least two weddings were performed there. At any time of year, the park can be a place of beauty and sanctuary, and for anyone. The fact that enjoying the riches of the park has nothing to do with how much money you have to spend makes it an increasingly rare urban jewel.

Washington Park can also be, increasingly, a place of grave danger. I know, firsthand, the perils of the park just as I know of its treasures. One unseasonably warm night in September, the one when Jennings was reelected so easily, I was beaten and robbed as I walked through the park, not far from where I live. Three teenagers, on bicycles, startled me and then ambushed me. In retrospect, the worst part of it, far worse than the physical pain that comes with being left at the mercy of three kids who have little of it to show, was the fear. After I was on the ground and they had my wallet and my money, I was whacked a few more times nonetheless. Why, I remember thinking, did these kids need to do that? What would they do next? Where and when would they stop? And now, I wonder, what absolute terror, so brutal and so unnecessary, Larry Omar Miller and Lamel Wells Robinson must have felt in those final moments of their lives. Why did these friends, one of whom leaves behind a 2-year-old daughter and was waiting to learn the results of his GED test, have to die the other day in the park?

The police are taking pains to say Washington Park is still safe. Safe, that is, within reason and safe when used with common sense. Just stay out of there after dark. It's the only thing they can say.

This holiday season, visitors keep coming to the park, almost always in the relative protection of their cars, to see the lights. It's the best thing they can do.

From the police to the public, the alternative is unthinkable. Lose that park and you've lost a city.

Editors' note: Four men were eventually arrested and charged in the killings of Larry Omar Miller and Lamel Wells Robinson. The victims had been randomly selected for a robbery as they walked through the park and were shot when they failed to produce money. Jesus Giovanni Lebron was sentenced to two consecutive life terms on first-degree murder and robbery charges; an appellate court unanimously upheld his conviction. Shamel Curry was convicted of second-degree murder and received a 50-year sentence. Aaron Bebo pleaded guilty to attempted second-degree robbery and testified against his companions. Justin Franklin was acquitted.

Drop This Case

Times Union editorial, April 27, 1998

The best that can be said about the arrest of an Albany bar owner on felony charges after he painted the curb in front of his building comes right from the top. First of all, says Mayor Jerry Jennings, there's no reason for John Diehsner to go to jail. This can be resolved in a less severe fashion, Mr. Jennings adds.

Indeed it can be. All Mr. Diehsner did, by his account and the authorities' as well, was try to keep cars from using his parking lot as a shortcut between Central Avenue and Clinton Avenue. There was yellow paint on the curb already, he said, so he added a fresh coat. The result was a tidier curb and a message to drivers to stop driving over it.

Only the city inferred a different message. It amounted to painting public property—and that apparently couldn't be tolerated. Mr. Diehsner was arrested earlier this month on a charge of felony-level criminal mischief. Yes, a felony, since the estimate of the damage to the repainted sidewalk exceeded $250. He was handcuffed, too, in full view of the customers in his bar.

More than anything, Mr. Diehsner is smarting over the humiliation of that experience. The police say, in essence, that the handcuffs come with getting arrested, in all but the most unusual circumstances. This case sounds mighty unusual to us, but the real point here is why did painting 25 feet of curb amount to a criminal matter in the first place?

Mr. Jennings says it would be easy enough for the city to remove the paint, since it bought equipment specifically for removing graffiti just last year.

It would be just as easy, in fact, to drop the criminal charges against Mr. Diehsner. Chalk it up to a misunderstanding and move on.

That should be the goal, at least. Mr. Diehsner's bar, JD's Playhouse, caters to a gay clientele. The police say that has nothing to do with his arrest, while Mr. Diehsner says it has everything to do with it. In a city that has made some laudable progress in its relations with the gay community, it would be a shame to reopen old wounds with overzealous police work. And in a city of 100,000 people, gay and straight alike, surely there are more pressing matters than how brightly the curbstones are painted.

Come Clean, Mr. Jennings

Times Union editorial, July 10, 1998

There's nothing surprising, nor subtle, about Albany Mayor Jerry Jennings's formal endorsement of Gary Domalewicz's candidacy for the state Assembly. Nor is there anything improper about it. The mayor has as much right to his preference as anyone else. Yes, it's a primary election in which Mr. Domalewicz is running. But in Albany, political struggles are more likely to be resolved in Democratic primaries than in general elections.

In that sense, primary campaigns can be good for the city as well as for the party. That was the case, in fact, when Mr. Jennings—running without any Republican opposition—won reelection last year in a primary against Jack McEneny.

That's state Assemblyman Jack McEneny, of course. As in Mr. Domalewicz's opponent.

Mr. Domalewicz made it clear that he was going after Mr. McEneny's Assembly seat the day after last September's mayoral primary.

It's been clear to us, certainly, that Mr. Jennings has wanted to see Mr. McEneny out of the Assembly ever since then. He was listed, at one point, as cochairman of a campaign fund-raiser for Mr. Domalewicz last fall. Then, for 24 hours or so this spring, Mr. Jennings was actually talking about running against Mr. McEneny himself—while continuing to serve as mayor, mind you.

Here's the problem with Mr. Jennings's endorsement of Mr. Domalewicz. Why does he deny that it has anything to do with retribution against Mr. McEneny?

Come on, Mr. Jennings. Level with the voters.

. . . A Defeat for the Machine

Times Union editorial, September 17, 1998

Wednesday was the day when Albany Democrats might have asked themselves if there's been enough payback. The pathetic attempt to oust Assemblyman Jack McEneny from office ought to be enough to convince even the die-hard elements of the old guard wistful for the days of retribution that it's time to move along.

Mr. McEneny's victory in Tuesday's primary election was even bigger than the one Mayor Jerry Jennings ran up in last year's primary. We point that out because this is Albany, and someone always is keeping score.

It's hard to imagine that Mr. McEneny would have faced such a challenge for reelection to the Assembly if he hadn't run against Mr. Jennings for mayor. It's harder still not to recognize Gary Domalewicz's unsuccessful campaign against Mr. McEneny as a telling rejection of the Albany axiom that in politics there must be punishment.

Primaries are healthy and even necessary in a one-party city. But they should be waged about issues, not personalities. They should be about thoughtful alternatives, not blind loyalty. A year later, Mr. McEneny's criticism of city government in Albany stands out, for the issues it raised and the hearing it received, as material for the civics books in contrast to the subsequent attempts by what's left of the city's Democratic machine to put him out of business.

Mr. Jennings would be wise to accept that. If the party is to accept the notion of conclusion, the mayor would do well to sign on as a coauthor.

As for Mr. Domalewicz, he had every right not to endorse Mr. McEneny as his party's nominee for a fourth term in the Assembly. But to insist that such an endorsement is dependent upon a further airing of their differences is to defy the reality and even the legitimacy of the election results. The votes have been cast, and the old ways have been rejected.

It's a different story to the north, south, and east of Albany. In the Republican primary in the sprawling 22nd Congressional District, the preferred candidate of the party bosses has prevailed. But the GOP voters have sent a message to their nominee, John Sweeney. If Mr. Sweeney won a majority of the vote, he did so only barely. His refusal to debate the issues with the other candidates clearly was a sticking point with many voters. It was hard to tell if his victory speech—complete with a call for a campaign "100 percent positive and 100 percent on the issues"— reflected a lesson heeded or an unintended irony.

In either event, Mr. Sweeney is not yet an incumbent. He should be aware of the risks of running like one.

A campaign in which Mr. Sweeney does debate Democratic nominee Jean P. Bordewich would be welcome indeed. Surely it would make the task of uniting the Republican Party easier. It might even prevent GOP leaders from having to face up to a new era, as the Albany Democrats must.

Albany's Hot-Dog Politics

Times Union editorial, April 5, 1999

Down by the state Capitol, it's the surest sign of spring. Inside, the finger-pointing is in full throttle as the budget is late once again. Outside, the food vendors are back along State Street, Washington Avenue, and Capitol Park. If only the heavy-handed politics could be properly kept indoors.

For the vendors, the cost of doing business in Albany has gone up. Almost doubled, if anyone is keeping score. The price of a cart license has jumped from $400 to $775. A truck license that used to cost $800 now goes for $1,550. Yes, it's the first increase in five years—a fact that most vendors readily acknowledge. But the sudden increase does raise questions about what sort of message the city is trying to send.

Even after paying for their licenses for this year, some of the 30 or so outdoor food vendors by the Capitol are worried about next year. They fear there won't be a place for them.

Why? To hear Mayor Jerry Jennings explain it, fewer vendors would result in better business for nearby restaurants. Think about that, though, and the mayor's idea doesn't make much sense.

It's hard to imagine the folks who settle on a hot dog or a sausage sandwich or a slice or two of pizza for lunch flocking to more expensive restaurants for a midday meal. Lunch for just a few bucks has a certain appeal.

Lunch in the park has some other advantages as well. On a warm and sunny day, it's hard to imagine an atmosphere as pleasant inside, well, anywhere. It's also quick. If your lunch hour only lasts, say, half that long, that's still plenty of time to spill out of the Capitol and the adjacent office buildings and grab something from a hot-dog cart. But it's not much time to go sit down someplace and be waited on.

That's not to say that the restaurants don't have a customer base of their own. A truly vibrant downtown, in fact, needs them. That's something even the vendors agree on. But the city should stay out of the noontime market and let it flourish under free-market competition.

City Clerk Nancy Anderson insists, meanwhile, that the only thing she and the mayor want to do to the vendors is spread them around town a bit more. The Corning Preserve has been mentioned as one place where the food carts could go. That's fine, as soon as a lunchtime crowd starts gathering there. But most people are working and congregating by the Capitol.

Mr. Jennings is determined to bring more people, and more jobs, to downtown Albany. He's succeeding, too. He just doesn't need to be so concerned with where all these people have lunch. A healthy city can accommodate sandwich vendors and fine eateries alike—and everything in between.

Justice for Ms. McEneny

Times Union editorial, May 7, 1999

Rachel McEneny's acquittal on a drunken-driving charge leaves this obvious yet troubling question: Why was such a weak case pursued as far as it was?

Ms. McEneny was arrested in the early hours of last September 16. The night of September 15 had been cause for celebration, certainly. Ms. McEneny's father, state Assemblyman Jack McEneny, had been victorious in the Democratic primary. But Ms. McEneny, his campaign manager, says she wasn't drunk. More to the point, a jury agreed.

This case unraveled almost immediately. The police failed to follow the proper procedure when they gave her a breathalyzer test. As a consequence, the test couldn't be used as evidence against her in court. More suspicious still is that the breathalyzer results clashed with a blood test taken at Albany Memorial Hospital two hours after Ms. McEneny's arrest. The police say her blood-alcohol content was 0.11 percent, which is legally drunk. The hospital says it was 0.04 percent, which is not.

Ms. McEneny would have had to sober up between the police station and the hospital at about twice the normal human rate for the cops' contention that she was drunk at the time of her arrest to hold up. That raises the possibility that she was sober all along.

It's impossible to stray very far from politics in wondering why this matter went all the way to a jury trial. Would someone less involved—or differently involved—in Albany politics have been prosecuted similarly? And would someone less savvy have known enough to get a blood test, and fight the DWI charges?

It's fair to ask as well just how relevant Mr. McEneny himself was to the case against his daughter. He has been, remember, critical of the police in the past. In his unsuccessful campaign for mayor of Albany in 1997, he maintained the city had a crime problem and that the police should be monitored by a civilian review board. His victory that night last fall was a rebuke to a political establishment that had tried to punish him for having run for mayor in the first place.

A grudge that should have been settled long ago instead carries over to new questions about how Albany works. The mishandling of what should have been such a routine matter does nothing to inspire confidence in either the city's police department or the county district attorney's office.

Driving while drunk is a very serious offense, of course. Some would argue that it is unsafe to drive after drinking even the limited amount of alcohol that Ms. McEneny acknowledges she had. But the sloppy and politically influenced application of the law is just as bad.

Time to Right a Wrong

President Bush Should Award the
Medal of Honor to Sergeant Henry Johnson

Times Union editorial, April 24, 2001

President Woodrow Wilson was the commander in chief of the American military forces all those years ago when Sergeant Henry Johnson, unable to serve with the Army overseas because he was black, fought so heroically with a New York National Guard unit assigned to a French regiment in World War I. Thanks to his storied valor, an enemy attack was turned back near Verdun on May 14, 1918. Sergeant Johnson's badly injured buddy, Needham Roberts, was saved and four enemy soldiers were killed.

Sergeant Johnson himself was seriously wounded, in more than 20 places. He returned home unable to resume his job as a railroad porter. He died destitute in Albany in 1938.

And still the indignities mount, so high and so egregiously that it's up to another commander in chief, President George W. Bush, to undo them. Mr. Bush must heed the persuasive advice of Senator Charles Schumer and Representative Michael McNulty. He must overrule the chairman of the Joint Chiefs of Staff, General Henry Shelton, and award Sergeant Johnson the Medal of Honor that he's been deprived of for nearly a century.

A campaign that began in Albany a decade ago to properly honor Sergeant Johnson should be nearing its fitting conclusion by now. In January, then–army secretary Louis Caldera recommended that Sergeant Johnson be posthumously awarded his medal at last. The rest should have been easy enough—routine approval at the Pentagon.

Instead General Shelton stands out as Sergeant Johnson's final adversary. He said no to Sergeant Johnson's medal, a most unusual act in itself, on these dubious grounds—that proper procedure wasn't followed. Recipients are supposed to be nominated within three years, and for verifiable acts.

Please. That means Sergeant Johnson would have had to be nominated by 1921—at a time when racism was a semi-official policy of the US armed forces. Does General Shelton truly expect that the same government that wouldn't permit Sergeant Johnson to fight abroad would have been prepared to give him its highest military honor?

Sergeant Johnson is being held to an unfair standard. Another black World War I veteran, a sailor named Freddie Stowers, was posthumously given the Medal of Honor in 1992 by a looser interpretation of the requirements. His award, though, came only after civil rights activists pressured Congress into investigating just why no African American soldier had been recommended by the military for the Medal of Honor prior to the Korean War.

As for verified instances of heroism, Sergeant Johnson's battlefield bravery was used in Army recruitment efforts. Isn't that good enough for General Shelton and the panel of generals that advised him? And what about the Croix de Guerre with gold palm, France's highest military honor, that Sergeant Johnson was awarded long ago. Doesn't that qualify as documented valor?

It is true that eyewitness accounts often accompany nomination for this honor. But that's not a remotely reasonable requirement more than 80 years after the fact.

Sergeant Johnson should not become a victim of rigid and bureaucratic thinking. If his undisputed heroism is the military at its best, then General Shelton's rationale for rejecting his medal is the military at its worst.

It's up to Mr. Bush to see the long struggle, first by Sergeant Johnson and then on his behalf, in the proper context. This is a president who spoke in his inaugural address just three months ago not only about prejudice but of hidden prejudice. Now comes the test. Commander in Chief Bush needs to ensure that a misguided general doesn't create a potentially ugly racial incident by denying honor to a man who deserves it by every imaginable standard.

Editors' note: Johnson was posthumously awarded the Medal of Honor by President Barack Obama on June 2, 2015.

Renewing Democracy Is Humbling

Times Union opinion piece, September 28, 2001

The ritual of proclaiming victory came without any buildup or much fanfare this time. Helen Desfosses stood before about three dozen people in her Rosemont Street living room the other night to tell them that all the votes were in, and yes, she had been effectively reelected president of the Albany Common Council. She didn't go on long at all before getting to what's still on everyone's minds, even in Albany and even on primary night. She said she was humbled by all that had happened, just like all politicians do at what has to be a rather heady dose of ego reinforcement. But surely she had to have meant it this time.

Albany hasn't changed, really, since the day two weeks ago when the same elections were to have been held. The issues that Desfosses was reelected on are no different. She wants to continue to be the city's ombudsman, and to lead the council on a more independent course. And she's determined to increase access in the city's poor and minority neighborhoods—where she didn't do so well, incidentally—to the Internet and related technology.

But the world around Albany has changed, and probably permanently. So a subdued gathering on primary night is how Albany, like so many other places, slowly moves ahead. The sanctity of an uptown neighborhood can be deceiving. Albany isn't that far from New York City, not that far from a place blown apart by terrorists. Desfosses's small gathering nonetheless had more than a few people with strong personal ties to the city and to its victims.

So the first person actually quoted—someone else's words, it seems, are invariably cited in these speeches—by Desfosses is the poet Carl Sandburg. He once said that each time a baby is born, we renew our very presence.

Desfosses says that each time an election is held, we renew our democracy. Voting, she continues, right now is like giving blood or donating money.

Only then did Desfosses get around to mentioning her opponent, Jim Coyne, who acknowledged two weeks ago that he had little fire for campaigning for local office with the nation on the brink of war. So goes primary night in a city where the players regard politics as Albany's only major league sport.

Desfosses wrapped up her speech with the promise that it will be different—livelier, she means, like it used to be—on this same night four years from now. And four years from what confronts us now.

By then, one of her supporters says, maybe she'll be running for mayor.

Maybe. Or maybe not. What matters far more is that on nights like that, in times like this, the mere notion of possibility is an empowering sentiment.

Jennings, Who Else?

Times Union editorial, November 4, 2001

Jerry Jennings is running for reelection Tuesday against three minor-party candidates, mostly well meaning, who are in no way qualified to be mayor of Albany. The vote of confidence Mr. Jennings deserves has been all but assured for some time. Anyone who might have run a credible campaign against him instead has endorsed him.

The issue is what sort of mayor Mr. Jennings might be in his third term. What he's accomplished, but also what he hasn't, offer some clues.

The mayor has succeeded in stabilizing the city's tax base, an impressive feat when Albany's population is declining. Finally some of the burden is off homeowners, taken up instead by the state—which owns so much of the property in the city.

Downtown is, without question, much more alive than it was when Mr. Jennings came into office. The entertainment district he envisions is well on to its way to completion. State government has more of a presence in the capital city. What Mr. Jennings needs to do now is make good on his determination to develop housing downtown, as well as to attract the retail business that has to come with it.

No longer is the police department something that city officials must so awkwardly rush to defend. Public Safety Commissioner John Nielsen has imposed a much more professional environment there. At last, there's a civilian review board in place to handle complaints against the police.

Achievements all, that should by no means be overlooked. What's likely to confront Mr. Jennings during the next four years, though, will be a good bit tougher. It will require more than the mayor's abundant confidence. Instead, better planning, and even more follow-through, will be needed.

Outside of downtown, too much of Albany shows signs of decline. Neighborhoods have been neglected. Delaware Avenue and lower Central Avenue, two business districts that Assemblyman Jack McEneny pointed to with alarm during the 1997 election, are, if anything, in worse shape four years later. City Hall's stepped-up code enforcement efforts too often seem to be no match for blight.

Arbor Hill, meanwhile, stands out for revitalization efforts that are now back at square one. The mayor's sense of what's best there, and in other minority neighborhoods as well, isn't enough. He needs to engage those communities and develop a consensus for what's the best way to make them more safe and more vibrant.

The other great concern for the city and challenge for its mayor is the public schools. The mayor is right when he cites schools, along with taxes, as the main reason why more people are moving out of Albany than moving in. Mr. Jennings's strong interest in the school system is natural enough. It's civic in nature but also personal as well. He made a career there before becoming mayor.

Mr. Jennings needs to better balance his determination that the schools improve with an acceptance that a good school system—from superintendent to school board—works best independently of City Hall. His insistence that he's taken little interest in who occupies either of those posts this election year is less than convincing.

It sounds quite daunting—providing stronger neighborhoods and creating the climate for better schools, and in an upstate city in a recessionary economy yet. Both, though, are within Mr. Jennings's capabilities.

He needs not only to raise his sights, but to sharpen them as well. His next term ought to be devoted as much to what can be done as to what should be done. It will be a time to deliver even more than he has already.

Joseph Sullivan, the Republican candidate; Elizabeth Pearson, the Green Party candidate; and Joe Laux, the Liberal Party candidate, have contributed little to a mayoral campaign that's been decidedly low-key. What's missing as a result has been a serious debate about the state of the city, and a closer examination of the mayor's record.

Come Wednesday, attention should turn to Jerry Jennings and an unfinished agenda for Albany.

Outsiders Defy Odds in Albany

Times Union opinion piece, November 10, 2001

Sometime Tuesday night, after the polls had closed and the results were coming in, it became apparent that grassroots Albany politics had changed a bit. They're more inclusive, it seems, less predictable, and perhaps more fun.

About two dozen or so people had gathered at Ristorante Paradiso on lower Central Avenue, a blighted area that's a legitimate campaign issue in its own right. They were with, or in two cases simply were, the victorious school board candidates Pat Fahy and Paul Webster. They were winning, only they didn't entirely believe it. It had been 11 years, and in another school board race, since a night quite like this.

In the restaurant that the movie version of William Kennedy's *Ironweed* had brought back from the dead, these two insurgents had defied themselves.

When it was time, Fahy spoke first. She stood at the center of a casually assembled circle in an otherwise dimly lit and quiet room. And she talked—quickly, nervously, excitedly. Under other circumstances, she is a focused, articulate, perhaps even slightly intense woman. But not this night. She was wide-eyed and jittery, getting a grip on the victory she had just pulled off.

Fahy was part of a team, with Webster, running a rather loosely organized and not very-well-financed campaign for the two open school board seats. Their platform was simple enough: That Albany either fixes its schools, academically as well as physically, or else loses even more of its population.

Their opposition was clear enough, too. Mayor Jerry Jennings and those allied with him had backed, for the most part, two other candidates—Paul Tenan and Dyan Parker, an incumbent. The issue there wasn't education, really. It's more a matter of control. Fahy and Webster have their own views about the appropriate influence of City Hall on the schools.

With that sort of opposition, Fahy figured, running for something as generally innocuous as the school board was playing hardball. There was a machine out there, she kept saying, in reference to the mayor and the support for the rival candidates. I'm from Chicago, she said more than twice. I lived with that my whole life, she said, mentioning the Daleys and their style of politics.

And now here she was in Albany, a resident for only four years, with more votes, easily, than any of the other four candidates. Happily, gratefully, she was trying to make sense of it all.

Webster spoke next. The same rather youthful countenance was there, all right, but with a touch of humility this time. He had run for office once before, for the Sixth Ward Common Council seat in 1997, and had lost. It took a moment for him to get his bearings in what now clearly was the winner's circle.

And then this. "The hip-hop generation has arrived."

Soon enough, he was talking, and in a cadence almost as rapid-fire as Fahy's, about just who he is and what this race meant to him. Webster's an outsider, too—born and raised in the same Long Island town as the band Public Enemy. So now there was a victory speech with rap lyrics. Rap lyrics and a refrain that might catch on, that is.

Webster was, he said, even less confident of winning this thing than Fahy when he started out. It's all about the kids, said the candidate who's quite upfront about his own political ambition. It's all about the kids, said the candidate who made a forceful case about the responsibility of the public schools to help stop the cycle of urban poverty.

On it went, before a crowd prone to a mild sort of activism, and one that knows more losses than wins. Even their victories this night came with the warning that two school board seats won't mean much of anything unless the $175 million school facilities plan is passed in a December 11 referendum.

The larger point there couldn't be missed, that it's up to the same people who just decided the school board election to make it pass.

The gathering was beginning to break up when word started to make its way back from the other end of the city, where Jennings was celebrating his reelection victory at Martel's restaurant at the municipal golf course. They knew about the school board outcome out there, it was said, and they weren't happy.

Whose City Is It?

Times Union editorial, May 10, 2002

Jerry Jennings brings to the job of mayor of Albany the refreshing qualities of accessibility and affability. He's clearly comfortable anywhere in the city, and in his own skin as well. The barriers between the mayor and the rest don't seem particularly daunting.

At least that's Mr. Jennings most of the time. It was another side of him that emerged a few days ago, and it wasn't very becoming.

"This is my city," the mayor declared, sounding rather like Louis XIV. Or was it Richard Daley I?

His anger is mostly directed toward the candidacy of Tom Keefe for City Court judge. He's running against the mayor's choices for the three judgeships in the September primary ballot, and with the support of Mr. Jennings's intra-party rivals, County Executive Michael Breslin and his brother, state Senator Neil Breslin.

It was in Mr. Jennings's city, across from, presumably, his City Hall in Academy Park, where Mr. Keefe announced his candidacy.

"Who are they to come in here and designate who the next City Court judge will be," Mr. Jennings demands to know.

Well, rivalries and tensions for control of The Party in a one-party city are one thing, and perhaps inevitably so. But let's keep it to a more or less egalitarian level.

It's the people's city, the people's park, and yes, the people's party. No one knows that better, or should, than Mr. Jennings, the old political maverick himself.

Albany has made some impressive strides under his leadership. The last thing it needs is an imperious or possessive mayor.

Albany's Anguish

Times Union editorial, January 3, 2004

When Albany awakened Thursday, to a new day and year, it was plainer than ever just how much the simple issues of law and order, and of crime and safety, had become the paramount concerns of an alarmed city. Twice in nine days, in locations not far from the core of the city's downtown and not more than a mile apart, decent, even noble, residents had fallen to gunfire. One, police lieutenant John Finn, was wounded and barely alive. The other, David Scaringe, 24, of the Center Square neighborhood, was dead.

Lieutenant Finn had been shot on December 23, trying to stop a criminal suspect. Mr. Scaringe had been killed on Wednesday afternoon, while police tried to pursue an unarmed criminal suspect. Across Albany, the casualties mounted, to include the city itself.

For the grim duty begins now, with scars ready to be ripped open not so deep beneath the surface, of a grand jury investigation to determine why it was that two officers who opened fire on a suspect in a motor vehicle stop gone wildly out of control had instead killed a bystander. The bustling intersection of Lark and State streets was where one tragedy compounded upon another, and yet another.

When Mr. Scaringe lay dying in the street, when the city was ready to begin its New Year's celebration, part of Albany was dying as well. He was so young, so bright (a Clarkson University–educated engineer) and so literally representative of urban hope. And now the city mourns him, and braces for the possible loss of so many more like him. It doesn't take gunfire to suck the life out of an aging but persevering city. Fear can do the trick as well.

Two police officers, Joseph Gerace and William Bonanni, confront the ultimate horror of simply rushing to a crime scene. Both fired their weapons, and one of them killed a man. The same system of law and justice that went awry on Wednesday must now determine if Mr. Scaringe's death was preventable, or if the officers acted justifiably. A city where crime claims too many victims must wait and wonder if one of its own should instead be alive today, under any reasonable standards for protecting the public safety. The police department's policy for such pursuits must now be reexamined and quite possibly changed.

Bystander dead, at Lark and State, on New Year's Eve. Pity the city.

Safety, and the fear for it, now surpasses the perception of how good the public schools are and the daunting task of sparing people from ever-higher property taxes as the biggest obstacle of all to keeping people in Albany. For to live here, or in any city, is to have certain reasonable expectations. For those like Mr. Scaringe, it's to walk down the street without walking into police gunfire. For Lieutenant Finn, it's that he can respond to a report of a bodega robbery without being felled by the bullet, allegedly, of a hardened criminal now on probation for a federal gun violation. For the more than 90,000 others, it's that they can live and work and escape either fate. For their tax dollars, they demand protection, not danger.

Today the city endures, of course, with its streets and buildings and its traffic and commerce, well intact. The city endures, but the city bleeds. A young resident is dead and doctors fight to keep a veteran cop alive. Either bleeding stops, or the city is ruined. A city is as healthy as those who roam its streets or enforce its laws. To lose Mr. Scaringe, and to pray for Lieutenant Finn, is to confront the dark prospects of a city with neither a soul nor a pulse.

Editors' note: Lieutenant John Finn died of his injuries at Albany Medical Center on February 12, 2004. Keshon Everett, charged in Finn's shooting, pleaded guilty to first-degree murder. In August 2004, he received a sentence of life in prison without the possibility of parole, plus 15 years on another weapons possession count. The City of Albany eventually paid $1.3 million to David Scaringe's family. For years after the shooting, people left flowers and candles on New Year's Eve as a makeshift shrine in Scaringe's memory at the corner of State and Lark streets, near where Scaringe lay dying in the street that afternoon. A grand jury narrowly cleared William Bonanni and Joseph Gerace of any wrongdoing. Both remained on leave for about two years. Gerace never returned to duty; Bonanni did return to duty and eventually retired.

It's All about the Guns

Times Union editorial, June 18, 2008

There's no one way to get guns off the streets of Albany and cities like it. And there's no point in endorsing one method over another. Whatever it takes, from enticement to lawful seizure, would seem to be the watchword after a 10-year-girl from Albany's West Hill was killed by a stray bullet late last month.

The arrest of a 15-year-old boy from the adjoining Arbor Hill neighborhood on murder charges drives the point home even further, especially after he allegedly told police the gun he fired in that fatal incident was, in effect, communal property at the Ida Yarbrough Homes.

So when the Reverend Charles Muller of Victory Church offers $150 gift certificates in exchange for turning in guns, what's not to applaud?

Maybe some of the guns will be legal ones, kept in secure circumstances and unlikely to have been used inappropriately. That's often the case with gun buyback efforts.

Other guns, though, might come much closer to the alleged description of the gun police say killed Kathina Thomas. The Reverend Muller thinks so, and who's to doubt someone who knows the community as well as he does? The point is to get the guns out of their usual hiding places. "A kid is going to hear about this and say, 'I want a new pair of Air Jordans,'" the Reverend Muller says. "They're going to come in. They're going to call me."

Now, in a simpler, more innocent time, a kid who yearned for a cool pair of sneakers might have mowed lawns, washed cars, delivered newspapers, or done some babysitting. But if someone is able to go shopping for basketball shoes at Crossgates Mall because he or she turned in a gun, that's one more lethal weapon taken out of the potentially wrong hands.

That's particularly notable in Albany, where 111 illegal guns were recovered last year, according to data from the federal Bureau of Alcohol, Tobacco, Firearms and Explosives. That's an increase from 81 in 2005. It's also five more guns than were confiscated last year in Yonkers, which has more than twice as many people as Albany does.

Those numbers also go against the trend in the ATF's Albany region. Illegal gun recoveries in those 18 counties dropped from 656 in 2006 to 533 last year.

There are those 111 guns, as Albany County District Attorney David Soares says, and then there are the people, mostly youths, who are all too inclined to use them. The battle goes on.

To think that new sneakers might make for safer streets. Or that more aggressive police work might do the same. Whatever it takes.

Editors' note: In November 2010, the Appellate Division of the state Supreme Court unanimously upheld the murder conviction of Jermayne Timmons, the teenager arrested in the shooting death of Kathina Thomas. Timmons was sentenced to 15 years to life in prison. The discovery that Timmons had fired a "community gun" that had been kept hidden for use by anyone who knew of its location led to the 2008 creation of the gun buyback program in Albany County referenced in this editorial. As of late 2017, the program was still in operation as a joint project of the Albany County district attorney's office and the Reverend Charles Muller of the Victory Church in Albany and had been credited with taking more than 650 guns out of the community.

Audit the Ghosts

Times Union editorial, January 20, 2009

The Albany Common Council is absolutely right to call for an independent audit of the cozy "ghost ticket" system that allowed police, their wives and girlfriends, and other favored citizens to park illegally with impunity.

It's this simple: The full story of this police exercise in favoritism needs to be told, and the police department is in no position to investigate itself on this one. The state comptroller's office, with a track record of responsible, objective municipal monitoring, is the right entity to do this.

If you were, say, too busy in traffic court or in line dutifully paying your parking fines to read about this, here's a quick recap: For years, the Albany Police Officers Union ran a program through which it handed out windshield stickers that looked like bull's-eyes. Parking enforcement officers who spotted illegally parked cars with the stickers would write bogus tickets that the drivers didn't have to pay. When the *Times Union* discovered the scheme, some top city officials, most notably Mayor Jerry Jennings and Police Chief James Tuffey, who was once president of the very union that ran the system, said they didn't know anything about it.

Mr. Tuffey has since pledged to implement a city-run system, under which such privileges would go only to those who ought to be getting them, such as police departments that need convenient access to government buildings downtown and off-duty police officers on official business, like testifying in court.

But this ghost ticket system needs a complete, objective airing. The department has been tainted by the revelation that the law in Albany is selectively enforced. And the city and its taxpayers have been ripped off, to the tune of untold hundreds of thousands of dollars, by both the people who had no valid reason to park illegally and their police enablers.

Among the many things the public is entitled to know: How did this get started? With whose blessing? How much money was lost? What safeguards, if any, were supposed to be in place to protect against fraudulent use? How and why did those safeguards break down?

Fully explaining and understanding the ghost tickets isn't about a witch hunt. It's about finding out how a presumably valid idea became corrupted, and understanding how to prevent that from happening again.

Jerry Jennings's Fifth Term

Opinion piece, special to the *Providence Journal*, Fall 2009

Election Day came earlier this month to this most ostensibly political of cities, where the pavement might as well have been poured and spread by the ward heelers, with all the authority of a rumor. It left with all the ferocity of a whisper.

Midday at the Corning Senior Center—remember that name—had the usual rush of voters reduced to such a trickle that one poll watcher couldn't help holding back her yawns. Nina Voss, matriarch of a downtown neighborhood and a longtime and loyal political foot soldier, wondered aloud when the voting would be done. Nina Voss, equally ardent Red Sox fan, wondered when the New York Yankees' inevitable recapturing of the World Series championship would at last be complete.

Around town, as the sun receded, the few lawn signs in the neighborhoods where in more contentious years they can sprout like dandelions instead suggested urban desolation more than civic engagement. The now-tattered placards stood out like the last of the summer weeds.

It was over before it began. Mayor Jerry Jennings won a fifth term without breaking his ever-familiar stride or deviating from his ever-recognizable script.

Jerry. The name's as ubiquitous here as Buddy would be in Providence. The similarities don't stop there, either. They do, fortunately, end right around where they should. Jennings is a capable, intense champion of an aging Northeastern city that needs that much and more. His prints are everywhere, both deservedly and needlessly. He's Cianci, but without the rug and without the rap sheet.

Tall, imposing, well-tailored, and even more self-confident, Jennings once summed up his style of leadership and management without a trace of irony or self-awareness.

"I don't want to hear that I don't listen to people," he said, so casually yet forcefully, to the Albany *Times Union* editorial board.

That was four years ago, as he was merely going for his fourth term. And, no, he hasn't really changed. He's more subdued on the surface, perhaps, but the same at the core.

Jerry Jennings rules here, but in Erastus Corning's shadow.

Yes, Jennings has been mayor for 16 years now. Corning, though, ran Albany, even more heavy-handedly than Jennings could ever get away with, for 42 years—from 1941 to 1983.

So there was the dud of November, and even a quick and then fizzled burst of intensity in the September primary. But high tide for the surges and bursts and unyielding commotion of Albany politics came in late October.

That was Corning's birthday. He'd have been 100 then. The enduring mayor—so charming, so disarming, and ultimately so unaccountable—was regaled anew. It was if he'd lived again, back from the periphery where in less ceremonious times yet more sentimental quarters he might as well have served as an absent yet influential committeeman or, perhaps, as an aging city commissioner not to be disturbed and not to be disrespected.

Erastus Corning 2nd. Think Claiborne de Borda Pell.

Think Pell, and then think deeper. Corning surely could match Pell, old dollar for old dollar, right down to the last drop of blue blood. He was Groton and Yale, of railroad money and a steel company fortune. Yet he was just as comfortable in the world of machine politics, Irish and working class, where votes were counted with the ferocity of another blood sport, cockfighting.

Corning brought a Waspy gentility, if not outright legitimacy, to the cronyism and corruption of his day. He simply preferred doing business with his friends, he said by way of explanation for insider deals. Snow removal so lackadaisical that it could have put other mayors out of business was OK, too, by the reasoning God put it there and God would, come spring, take it away.

Times change, of course. The people in Albany—they're here; believe me—who'd like to run things the Corning way know better. Still, the former mayor's presence is subtle, perhaps, but eternal. The political year began with an upstate congresswoman named Kirsten Gillibrand appointed to what had been Hillary Clinton's Senate seat. Gillibrand is the granddaughter of Polly Noonan, who had been an aide to Corning, every bit as close, and maybe even closer, to him as his wife. It was a relationship that left the newspapers delicately describing her role as his "confidante." It was the Noonans, not the Cornings, to whom the mayor left his vast estate. New York's new senator had Albany's legendary mayor back in the news.

As for Jennings, he was more of a bit player this election night, when the bigger local political story came in an adjoining suburb. He looked nonetheless dignified enough, even stately, in sharp contrast to a 1977 photo with Corning, reprinted in the author Paul Grondahl's biography, *Mayor Corning*, in which he looks as if he's dressed for a night at a disco.

Jennings is 62 now, and just a bit weathered. He shows no interest at all of letting anyone else be mayor. His biggest race is one against time. He'll begin his fifth term on January 1, ever mindful that Corning was in his 11th term when he died, still in office. He can't be thinking of that long a run. Or can he?

Editors' note: In May 2013, Jerry Jennings announced that he would not seek a sixth term, bringing to a close his 20 years as Albany's mayor. Albany City Treasurer Kathy Sheehan won the Democratic mayoral primary September 10, 2013, six days after Jim died. Given that Albany had not elected a Republican to a city office in decades, Sheehan's primary victory effectively guaranteed her election in November 2013. She won a second term in November 2017. Jim had expected her 2013 victory and had insisted that the most interesting aspect of Sheehan's likely tenure as mayor would not be her status as the city's first female leader, but the fact that Sheehan, who was born in Chicago, would be the first mayor of Albany who was not a native of the city.

Memories of Larks at a Tavern

Times Union opinion piece, May 6, 2011

A year ago today, when I wasn't yet quite awake, the phone rang. It was early enough to be bad news or, better yet, a wrong number.

It was my friend Teddy. There had been a fire, not long before dawn, a few blocks away at the Lark Tavern.

We had been there just the night before, the regular gang of us. It was Cinco de Mayo, spring at last upstate, and we laughed and talked and sipped margaritas into the twilight.

The Lark hasn't been open since. The fire was bad enough to be big local news for days. It was all there, as stories go—a prominent Albany landmark, an enduring business that opened just as Prohibition was lifted, operated most recently by a revered woman-about-town, Tess Collins.

And then came the condolences. In the newsroom, by email, and over the phone. Even from my mother-in-law in Connecticut.

I had been known to, ah, stop by the Lark. I wouldn't doubt that I was there two nights before the fire, too. I first went there, I well recall, on my first day in town. It was a warm afternoon in October of 1985. I sat at the bar, going through the classified ads in the *Knickerbocker News*, looking for a place to live and using the pay phone to call about a few.

Not the first bar, not by a decade or so, that I ever liked. Just the best. Spacious, with high ceilings and a classic tile floor. Bright, too, as bars go, with sunlight streaming in through windows that brought in the street life of Madison Avenue. And utterly unpretentious.

Taverns tend to have their own culture, daunting to anyone not part of the regular clientele. They're about drink, and maybe food. But they're just as much about conversation, camaraderie, and belonging.

The Lark was the place that was always open late, well after the night shift. I could cash my paycheck there, at an hour when the banks were just a rumor. Billy Gannon, who ran the place in those days, could spot an hour of overtime halfway down the block.

It's where I became friends with a guy by arguing well past midnight about the first US war in Iraq. It's where I first called, on that same pay phone, the woman who's now my wife.

More recently, on the day shift, it was the perfect interlude between work and supper. Leave it to Jimmy Breslin, the great writer and long-ago drinker, to say it best: "There's nothing better than going to a bar and lying to your friends."

For months after the fire, the question was the same. Where do we go now?

Say what you will about Albany—and I have, on these very pages. But there's no shortage of spots.

We've found other places. Everything tastes the same.

What is different is what's become of us. Our lives, I guess, aren't so unlike a night at a tavern—at different times so endearing, so sad, and sometimes just innocuously similar to the one before it.

Teddy graduated from law school and just passed the bar exam. Howard married Josephine. Joey's about to watch another of his daughters graduate from college.

Johnny died, and way too young. Matt's company transferred him to the Boston area.

Timmy still writes arts criticism for the paper. Paul continues his career in state government. His brother Bob, an artist and carpenter, is back in Albany. Kurt is still a professor. Patrick works at Tess's new place, downtown, while she's in a fight to reopen uptown. I still go home to Darryl, to whom Tess once said that I never "look around."

We'll be together again somewhere, most of us, soon enough. Until then, raise one for your own favorite spot. It might mean more to you than you realize.

POLITICS

Jim's friend, former *Times Union* editorial cartoonist John DeRosier, drew this cartoon to mark the inauguration of President George W. Bush in January 2001. John put caricatures of Jim (second from right, under "The cartoonists") and himself (far right) into the drawing and inscribed the original to Jim after the cartoon ran in the *Times Union*. Reprinted by permission of the *Times Union*.

Introduction

Jim McGrath Loved Politics

Howard Healy

I first learned of Jim's death after my Thursday morning commute into work in downtown Albany, where I noticed all the flags were at half-staff. I remember asking myself who was being mourned—a national figure, a state or local leader? As I would soon find out when I turned on my email, it was Jim, who had died suddenly Wednesday while vacationing at Cape Cod. Yes, the same Jim McGrath who never spared his pen when it came to holding City Hall accountable for its lapses. How was it, then, that Jim had earned such an extraordinary tribute from those he had so often challenged?

The answer, I think, is that while Jim may have covered politics from the outside, he knew politics from the inside out. From his earliest days, he had witnessed politics as a whole, the good and bad, the gray areas, the competing interests, the compromises—and, above all, the power to set things right. For a youngster growing up in Boston in the shadow of Democratic lions like the Kennedys and Tip O'Neill, and a City Hall with deep Democratic roots in the old Irish neighborhoods, how could it have been otherwise? Jim witnessed politics and power again and again in his short life. After Boston, he went away to college, in Lake Forest, Illinois, right next door to Mayor Daley's Chicago. Daley, Chicago, politics—they're all synonyms. And, of course, when Jim wound up in Albany, he saw politics in full once again. Like Boston and Chicago, Albany had its share of Democratic lions, with names like Moynihan, Corning, and Cuomo, and a City Hall long dominated by Democrats.

By the mid-80s, though, when Jim arrived here, the cracks in the Albany Democratic machine were beginning to show—so much so that by the early 90s, City Hall would be occupied by a self-styled maverick Democrat, Jerry Jennings. Others within the party's ranks would ultimately strike independent paths as well, and Jim championed them all, provided they had something to offer in the way of making life better in the city. But he was never a scold. He knew well the problems Mayor Jennings faced with crime (Jim himself was mugged once in Washington Park) and blighted neighborhoods and increasingly sparse state aid—an awareness that gave his editorials and commentary insight, breadth, and balance. Yet he was relentless when it came to exposing cronyism and corruption, whether in city or county circles or the state Capitol. Read his searing critique of the politicians and lawyers who arranged a lesser plea for an Assembly staffer accused of rape. Read the transcript of an interview Jim had with the Canadian Broadcasting Corporation after the downfall of Governor Eliot Spitzer, who had boldly promised reform only to become entangled by the corrupting influences of power, money, and sex.

Jim's canvas wasn't confined to Albany. He was one of the first journalists in New York to come to the defense of John O'Hara as he struggled against what had all the appearances of payback politics played by Brooklyn's then–district attorney Charles Hynes. Jim was a superb observer of the delicate and divided loyalties that many New Yorkers felt when fellow New Yorker Hillary Clinton was battling a newcomer named Barack Obama for the Democratic presidential nomination. And those "troubles" in Northern Ireland? Jim produced masterful analyses of the political complexities underlying that long struggle. In the view of many *Times Union* readers with Irish roots, Jim was too evenhanded. But those critics argued with emotion; Jim argued with reason.

Above all, Jim gave voice to those who were so often ignored by those in power. Whenever I read his editorials and his op-ed commentary, I can hear that voice again, Jim's conscience again, speaking for the powerless, the politically disenfranchised. No matter that his words are in cold print, when you read them, you too will hear his voice, one that commands attention. It will not fade. It will not diminish over time.

LOCAL

Preaching to the Faithful

Times Union feature story, March 17, 1995

Sinn Fein leader Gerry Adams arrives at Albany's Hibernian Hall for a sermon of peace

On an otherwise dreary Sunday night in March, Albany is Gerry Adams's town. First stop of the victory tour, as the slogan on the T-shirts for sale is calling it.

The crowd begins to gather outside the Hibernian Hall on Quail Street even before the doors are open and hours before he speaks. Adams is probably still in New York City at this point, and the simple anticipation of a visit by the leader of Sinn Fein, who two years ago couldn't even get a visa into this country, will rival the event itself.

It's an older crowd for the most part, and many people look like they're dressed for church. Lots of green, of course: green neckties, green sweaters, at least one green blazer (worn by a fellow who looked more than a little bit like Tip O'Neill), and at least one green windbreaker, worn by a fellow with a green cap that says, "Schenectady AOH." There's also at least one person wearing an IRA button.

The beer, domestic and Guinness in plastic cups, is flowing pretty well, and nobody seems shy about smoking cigarettes. The banter runs from the practical to the casual to the mildly political. The wife of the president of the Albany Hibernians is politely telling a woman wearing a sash of the three colors that, no, they won't be serving coffee later. "Anyone driving will just have to drink responsibly." There's lots of "hihowareya" and "a great night for Albany, isn't it?" Someone else says, "We're all Republicans (as in Irish Republicans) tonight."

Adams is the leader of the political wing of the Irish Republican Army, which has been fighting, seemingly forever, often by outright terrorism, to free the six counties of Northern Ireland from British rule. He's an intriguing figure under any circumstances, and especially so now that the IRA and the Protestant extremists of Northern Ireland have held to a cease-fire for going on seven months now. He represents a cause long popular in Albany and suddenly more legitimate in Washington.

It doesn't take long for about 600 people to fill the hall, a down-on-its-heels sort of place, decorated with everything from a crucifix to a huge Jameson's St. Patrick's Day banner to an altar of sorts to St. Patrick himself.

The anticipation builds, and the atmosphere shifts from church hall bingo night to the scene before a rock concert. Lots of people know each other, and the Irish American activists and the local Democratic pols are pretty easy to spot. There's nothing skeptical or contentious about this crowd. Adams will speak to the faithful tonight.

There's an announcement that he is in Albany now—actually, he's driving up in a minivan with a couple of off-duty Albany cops and getting the full police escort treatment—and will be at the hall in 20 minutes.

They start clearing the aisles, getting ready for his entrance. The TV cameras seem more noticeable now, and the music, from Irish traditional to Van Morrison, is blaring. Finally, the waiting, from a few hours to more than a few years, depending on how you keep track of such things, is over and a burly bagpipe band leads Adams to the front of the hall. There's a final rush for the seats and then people are standing on their chairs.

Gerry Adams, once a political prisoner in his own land and once banned from this land, is in Albany, at the Hibernian Hall, right underneath the green and white crepe paper hanging from the ceiling, and right before their eyes.

"Gerry! Gerry!" the crowd chants, hands clapping, as Adams takes his seat on a tiny platform, along with Mayor Jerry Jennings and a host of others.

"He looks a little tepid," a woman in the first row says, and it turns out that she's right. Adams has the flu and later jokes that he didn't have it when he left Belfast and must have picked it up flying over London.

Just about kickoff. A fellow with a remarkably good voice and no music supporting him belts out the traditional Irish national anthem, "A Soldier's Song."

"Soldiers are we, who've pledged our lives to Ireland," the anthem goes. Many, maybe even most of the faithful, know the words and sing along heartily. Adams sings too, but with less vigor. With the anticipation rivaling the event, he has less to anticipate.

When he does speak, it's in Irish as well as English. The words are clear and thoughtful, spoken in a heavy accent. This is the real thing that the faithful are hearing. It's an understated eloquence, and Adams is probably the most controlled person in the hall at this point.

He takes a dig or two at the Brits, but this is a conciliatory speech that stresses peace and not violence.

For the faithful, it's a sermon more than a pep talk: "We are talking about peace between all the people of Ireland. The Protestant people of Northern Ireland are our brothers and sisters. They are part of what we are. We are trying to make peace with a part of our own people."

He talks, as well, of his hopes for Ireland, of redistributing its wealth and of a nation with a strict separation of church and state. He gets great applause, at least from women, when he speaks of an Ireland free of sexism.

The music blares again, briefly, before Adams takes a few questions. One woman wants to know if she can give him an envelope with a donation.

"Now that's an easy one," Adams answers.

Indeed it is. Fund-raising, with President Clinton's approval even, is a big part of this trip.

Time was, until a week ago, that Sinn Fein was banned from raising money in the United States. The money, the reasoning went, would go for violent, not peaceful, purposes. Now, with the momentum that the cease-fire brings, there's less suspicion in Washington of Adams and his motives.

The flu aside, it's an easy night. If Gerry Adams can't make it here, at the Albany Hibernian Hall, he can't make it anywhere. This is a man who has gone from the US State Department blacklist to assuming a crucial role in pursuing peace, lasting peace, in Northern Ireland. Adams basks gracefully in the affection of Albany, but the diplomacy and the politics ahead are the real test.

Then after a quick news conference, he's gone, leaving behind his best wishes for today, St. Patrick's Day. Adams will be at the White House today with Clinton, far from the 20-bucks-a-head crowd at the Albany Hibernian Hall. The crowd lingers, though, even after Adams leaves.

The music is still playing and the bar is still open. Many people back in Ireland see Adams's US tour as nothing more than the latest move in a chess game, but in Albany, for the hometown crowd that takes its ethnic politics seriously, these are heady times.

In a corner of the room, near the bathroom door, an earnest-looking man says, without being asked, "A great night and a long time coming."

All Eyes on Albany

Times Union editorial, December 22, 1999

The perception that it would be impossible—too much attention in the press, emotions off the meter—to conduct a fair trial in the Bronx for four white police officers accused of murder in the death of an unarmed West African immigrant is, by the decree of a state appeals court, reality. The test of the judicial system moves here, to Albany County.

But already there's this perception as well, that Albany is the wrong place, too far and too different, from the rugged urban terrain where Amadou Diallo died to conduct this trial. The inevitable sense of suspicion anytime police go on trial heightens considerably. The argument that a predominantly black county would be irreparably biased against the police turns on its head. The perception now persists in some quarters in New York City that a predominantly white county will be biased in favor of the officers and inhospitable to out-of-towners, minorities mostly, demanding that the police be held accountable.

The burden of Albany County, then, is as clear as it is enormous. It's to dispel such perception, and to convey the reassuring reality that Albany can handle what New York City has been spared.

Downstate, and beyond, is watching. There are the digs in the big-city press, of course, suggesting this is a rural outpost few of us would notice. Silly, surely, but still harmless. But there's also the serious suggestion that a change of venue for a case with such heavy racial overtones puts New York, in the words of one columnist, that much closer to Simi Valley and Rodney King.

The unappealable court ruling that the trial must be moved comes down, ultimately, to a hastily drawn conclusion that 12 impartial jurors could not have been found in all of the Bronx, which happens to have four times the population of Albany County. A credible jury must reflect, at the very least, the limited racial diversity—compared to the Bronx—that does exist here. An all-white jury, like the one in the trial of two Albany police officers acquitted of beating Jermaine Henderson, would send the worst-imaginable message. Adequate minority representation is the shared responsibility of a yet-to-be-selected white local judge, rather than the black female presiding judge in the Bronx, and out-of-town prosecutors and defense lawyers alike.

A fair and orderly trial overall is the responsibility of the entire state of New York. But it will rest most prominently on the presumably ordinary citizens of Albany and its suburbs, called upon to act as the peers of the New York City police force. It will be up to them to make sense of why Mr. Diallo was shot 41 times after apparently failing to heed a call to halt in the vestibule of his apartment building.

All that will take place in the confinement of the county courthouse, just a couple of blocks from the state Capitol, where legislators have seen to it that cameras are barred from courtrooms. A case that's generated so much attention and interest as to require moving it 150 miles away just might be what it takes to force the public's access to the criminal justice system to be reopened.

Some of those with the most intense interest in the outcome of a trial that's primarily about the political culture of New York City will be in Albany. For them, distance won't be a deterrent. Observers, and indeed activists, will be in the courthouse and on the streets, too. The demonstrations promised already are another opportunity for Albany to manage what the appellate judges were convinced New York could not. In that sense, Mayor Jerry Jennings and Police Chief John Nielsen will face a trial of their own. Again, the burden will be easy to recognize but harder to overcome: Erase any perception that the city is ill-equipped to accommodate the scrutiny and tensions that the trial with bring with it.

It's impossible to imagine an outcome of a trial that has yet to begin that won't stir cries of justice not served. But none of those cries need to reflect on where the trial was held and who sat in judgment. Albany County's burden is Albany County's challenge. It's best to assume everyone is watching.

Editors' note: In February 2000, an Albany County jury of four black women, one white woman, and seven white men acquitted all four officers on all charges against them. The trial judge allowed cameras into the courtroom during the testimony of witnesses, in an exception to New York's ban on such coverage. The rules regarding cameras in the courtroom have since been clarified to make clear that the sitting judge has wide discretion on camera coverage.

Uneasy Justice

Times Union editorial, December 29, 2003

There's good reason to be troubled today about how justice was dispensed in a case last week in Albany County. Just six months ago, J. Michael Boxley, the former chief counsel to Assembly Speaker Sheldon Silver, was arrested in the state Capitol; he later was indicted on four felony charges of raping a 22-year-old legislative aide. Last Monday, that was reduced to a single misdemeanor count of sexual misconduct.

Mr. Boxley admitted, in court and under oath, that he had sexual intercourse with the woman against her will. For that, he avoids even a day in prison. Mr. Boxley instead will be placed on probation for six years, must register as a sex offender, and must pay a $1,000 fine. He still enjoys his personal freedom, though he could have been sentenced to a year in jail on the conviction. He might very well be able to continue to practice law.

District Attorney Paul Clyne's handling of the case invites some questions. Last June, he joined in the public spectacle of Mr. Boxley's arrest and subsequently obtained an indictment on charges including first-degree rape. All that was no doubt influenced by the fact that Mr. Boxley had been accused in a similar case of sexual assault two years ago, by a woman who decided not to press criminal charges. An Assembly investigation was halted at the request of both parties, and there were no sanctions against Mr. Boxley.

But why, in the end, did the district attorney allow this case to be plea-bargained down so far? Did he, as his subsequent actions suggest, not have such a strong case after all? There's something unsettling about Mr. Clyne's office asking that the rape charges be dismissed in favor of the misdemeanor plea because of the difficulty of trying and proving the case.

There were, of course, obstacles to consider before going to trial. Mr. Boxley's victim was hesitant to go through the subsequent ordeal of testifying against him. And she now says she has no regrets about allowing Mr. Boxley to avoid going to jail. Her intention is to start the next year with all this behind her. That's understandable, but not necessarily consistent with the duty of a district attorney to pursue justice when he or she sees fit.

Mr. Clyne's actions aren't the only ones open to question. Perhaps most offensive of all is the assertion by Mr. Boxley's lawyer, E. Stewart Jones, that he let an innocent man plead guilty only to avoid the dangers of having a black man stand trial before a white jury. Such a statement can betray prejudice, if not outright racism, of its own.

If Mr. Jones was so concerned about a fair trial for Mr. Boxley, he should have sought a change of venue. Further, if Mr. Jones is so convinced that his client wasn't guilty, not of anything, why did he allow him to admit to such a serious offense? Mr. Boxley is now a convicted sexual offender as a result. He need not be a racial martyr.

NEW YORK

A Voting Outrage

Times Union editorial, May 19, 2001

New York's highest court has a chance to clarify just what constitutes residency under state election laws. Mundane as it sounds, the matter is critical for a Brooklyn political maverick named John Kennedy O'Hara, who's fighting a felony conviction for illegal voting.

That's right, voting. Mr. O'Hara stands, apparently, as the first person since Susan B. Anthony—convicted for trying to vote before women obtained that right—to be found guilty of such an offense. Bizarre as it sounds, the implications are scary for anyone else who might run for office or deem to vote for someone who does.

Where someone lives and where he or she votes used to be a loosely defined and loosely enforced matter in this state. It was fine, the Court of Appeals said in a civil case ruling 29 years ago, when John Holt-Harris was elected to a city judicial position in Albany from an address where he recalled sleeping only once in seven years.

In the only other criminal case involving voting residency in New York, a man named Benjamin Ramos, running for a Bronx school board seat, was arrested and charged with registering and voting from a place that did not qualify as his residence under the election laws. His indictment was overturned in a decision that was upheld by the state's second-highest court in 1994. The prevailing reasoning was that a candidate can choose a residence that isn't a primary or principal residence for the purpose of voting so long as it is not a sham address.

Which brings New York to Mr. O'Hara. Three times he's stood trial, on felony accounts, for illegal voting and false voter registration. The Brooklyn district attorney's office maintains the crime occurred in 1992 and 1993. Before then and since then, five times in all, Mr. O'Hara has been an unsuccessful candidate for both the state Assembly and the New York City Council, running against the Brooklyn Democratic organization.

Mr. O'Hara doesn't deny registering and voting from an address on 47th Street in Brooklyn—an ex-girlfriend's residence, as it happens, where he occasionally stayed and which he used as an address while he ran for a redistricted City Council seat, even though it wasn't legally required. Some of his personal financial records from that time listed the 47th Street address, and neighbors attested that he sometimes stayed there. All the while, Mr. O'Hara says, he kept his other residence, on nearby 61st Street in Brooklyn. The district attorney's office, though, says 61st Street was the only place he lived—and that 47th Street never met the standard of a principal residence where he had always intended to return.

Suddenly the matter of maintaining two residences, not uncommon in New York politics and upheld as legal in a 1983 Court of Appeals decision, wasn't so readily accepted. Yes, Mr. O'Hara had two residences, but neither was a sham.

Since his arrest in 1996, Mr. O'Hara has been disbarred as an attorney, lost his right to vote, ordered to pay $20,000 in fines and restitution, and perform 1,500 hours of community service.

His plight is one more reason why residency laws should be made simpler and enforced consistently. The appropriate dismissal by the Court of Appeals of the case that's come to haunt him would allow Mr. O'Hara to go on with his life, other New Yorkers to vote and run for office without fear of such prosecution, and Susan B. Anthony to stand properly alone in history.

Editors' note: In January 2017 and following a reinvestigation of his case by the Brooklyn district attorney's office, a state court judge cleared O'Hara's conviction from his record. Charles Hynes had lost his bid for reelection in 2014, and his successor, Kings County district attorney Kenneth Thompson, had reopened the investigation into the charges against O'Hara as part of an ongoing review of a number of convictions obtained during Hynes's tenure. In that reinvestigation, a key witness used by Hynes completely revised the testimony she gave during the original case prosecuted by Hynes, opening the path to O'Hara's exoneration. Thompson died of cancer before he could follow through on clearing O'Hara's name, but his successor, Eric Gonzalez, completed the reinvestigation and recommended that the conviction be cleared. In January 2017, O'Hara filed a $25 million federal lawsuit for malicious prosecution against Hynes and former state Assembly Member James Brennan of Brooklyn, whom O'Hara accused of colluding with Hynes as payback for O'Hara's political activism and insurgency against the established Brooklyn political order. As of the publication of this book, that lawsuit is still active.

Voter Beware

Counterpunch.org opinion piece, November 8, 2005

It's Election Day, and I can't stop thinking of John Kennedy O'Hara, whose sad and bizarre tale in the polling places and the courtrooms of New York ought to be a warning to all Americans. His story is simple: O'Hara, who grew up and lives still in Brooklyn, New York, was a good citizen. He voted in every election he was eligible to vote in since the age of 18—it was a point of pride for a once geeky civics student who when he was just 11 years old handed out fliers for George McGovern—and as a young man he tried to run for office, tried to better the system. Five times he ran unsuccessfully, for the New York City Council and the New York State Assembly. As thanks for his effort, the earnest kid became, on the cusp of middle age, a disbarred attorney and convicted felon, an official second-class citizen whose future had been seemingly forever darkened. And the decade-long prosecution in the case of *People v. O'Hara* now has some chilling ramifications for each of the 11 million or so people eligible to vote today across New York. It means they, like O'Hara, could face felony prosecution for stepping into a voting booth. In fact, anyone who might vote anywhere in the United States today could find themselves with a prosecutor on their tail.

It's been four and a half years since I came to know O'Hara, a one-time rising Wall Street lawyer who at 44 is now bankrupted and jobless. When in April 2001 he telephoned my office in the editorial page department of the Albany *Times Union*, the paper of record in the state capital, he was alternately articulate and earnest, desperate and incredible, at once deadly serious about his plight and unable to keep from laughing at its absurdities. It turned out this stranger on the phone, who reassured me this wasn't some crazy hoax, had clashed with the Democratic bosses in Brooklyn just often enough that the bosses had to make an example of him. His most unforgivable act of rebellion in the backbiting world of Brooklyn machine politics was to demand in court that the US Department of Justice step in and order the suspension and rescheduling of the Democratic primary election in 1996. The '96 voting, such as it was, had been a fiasco, with tens of thousands of voters disenfranchised. Voting machines throughout Brooklyn arrived as late as ten hours after polls were supposed to open. The *Village Voice* called it "the worst electoral debacle in modern city history," and a federal judge reviewing the case—finally ordering a new election—wondered whether the election had been purposely stolen (much as some people still suspect, with no small supply of evidence, that those 20 electoral votes at stake in Ohio last year were similarly commandeered). It was a lawsuit by O'Hara that brought about a new election. His heroism left him more of an enemy than ever to the Brooklyn establishment. An aide to Brooklyn state Assemblyman James Brennan, a particular nemesis of O'Hara's, told a reporter seven years later, "John O'Hara deserved some sort of street justice; that's what a lot of people wanted to mete out." A month after the electoral debacle of September of 1996, O'Hara was indicted. The same aide to Brennan tried to defend the indefensible this way: "If there was anybody who should have been selectively prosecuted, it was John Kennedy O'Hara."

His arrest had come at the hands of Brooklyn District Attorney Charles "Joe" Hynes, a powerhouse prosecutor who served Brooklyn's political bosses. The charge was a strange one: O'Hara had voted from what prosecutors contended was an illegal residence. It was the address of his then girlfriend, 14 blocks away from an apartment he'd kept for almost 25 years. O'Hara says, to this day, that he was effectively, and legally, living in both apartments. But he was voting from just one of them. The evidence backed that up, with financial records and testimony from neighbors attesting that he frequently stayed at the address in question. The district attorney's office, however, insisted that the girlfriend's address was a sham that failed to meet the legal standard of a "principal and permanent residence to which [he] had always intended to return," as the court record put it.

A five-year ordeal of conviction, reversal, reinstatement, and appeal—three trials in all—left O'Hara guilty of a felony, stripped of his license to practice law (his means of survival), fined $20,000, sentenced to five years' probation, and 1,500 hours of community service. He had been reduced by political attrition to a life that only faintly resembled all that he had aspired to through college and law school and his rebellious, abortive career as a politician.

On that April day of 2001, O'Hara was making his pitch to me at the editorial board—a common enough act of last resort—because his case was pending before the highest court in New York, the oddly and perhaps misleadingly named Court of Appeals. O'Hara took a special delight in pointing out that he was the first person to be successfully prosecuted for illegal voting in New York since 1873. His compatriot in crime, he gleefully told me, was Susan B. Anthony.

O'Hara's story checked out. So the *Times Union* ran with an editorial urging the court to stop an abuse of justice that had rendered what was unbelievable into something unforgivable. The editorial boards of the *New York Daily News* and the *New York Sun*—not exactly papers itching to side with the likes of O'Hara against an often-vengeful prosecutor like Hynes—followed with denunciations of the case. Even *Harper's Magazine* published an 8,000-word cover story on O'Hara's saga.

But O'Hara's plea to the high court fell on deaf ears among the justices at the Court of Appeals, who, incredibly, upheld his conviction. Since then, the injustice has been magnified by the indifference to it. The *New York Times* editorial page has never said a word about him. Neither Howell Raines nor his successor as editorial page editor, Gail Collins, appear the least bit troubled that the precincts of Brooklyn are home to a political prisoner.

Today, O'Hara fights on, in a struggle ever more daunting. The setbacks accumulate—the Supreme Court declined to hear the case in January of 2004, and a New York state judge last month rejected his claim of selective prosecution—while his legal options erode. O'Hara is left paying his public penance cleaning out garbage cans in a city park, across the street from where he went to high school and unrecognized by the people whose votes he used to seek.

Election day, of course, is depressing enough, given the miserable voter turnout and the near 100 percent incumbency of so many legislatures (the worst example probably being the US Congress). O'Hara's case makes it even more so. Today marks one more election in which O'Hara can't vote. It's an indignity that rivals any other miserable lesson about American politics.

When I last interviewed O'Hara, in September, two things stood out in the kitchen of his apartment. There was the usual pile of weeks-old and months-old beer cans, and there was a voting notice from the New York City Board of Elections. The city government still had him on the list of citizens entrusted with enfranchisement.

O'Hara could legitimately be among those voters, if only he'd given in just a bit. Indeed, *People v. O'Hara* could have been plea-bargained down to a misdemeanor and would today be long-settled and forgotten. But O'Hara felt that he had no choice but to stand his ground. He couldn't stomach the example he'd otherwise be setting. What might DA Hynes and the corrupt elected officials he served do next?

O'Hara's legacy, of one legal defeat after another, carries its own legal precedent, of course—one that goes well beyond Brooklyn. Clearly, voters can now be prosecuted anywhere in New York State, if they can't prove something as chimerical as a "principal and permanent residence." By refusing to hear O'Hara's case, the Supreme Court brought national implications to his plight. What happened in New York conceivably could happen elsewhere.

Bennett Gershman, a Pace University law professor, recognized as much two years ago as O'Hara awaited word of his last-ditch appeal. The lesson for anyone involved in the political system in New York, he said, is "there but for the grace of God go I."

The polling place where I vote in Albany is not more than a few blocks from the state capitol where he had hoped to serve. Such aspirations have left him, at just 44, a battered man.

If that doesn't frighten you, what does?

Transcript of *As It Happens* Interview
on Eliot Spitzer's Resignation

Aired via the Canadian Broadcasting Corporation, March 12, 2008

JANE HAWTIN, HOST

Hawtin: Jim McGrath is the chief editorial writer for the Albany *Times Union*. We reached him in Albany. Hello, Jim.

McGrath: Hello!

Hawtin: Jim, was there ever any doubt that Eliot Spitzer would have to resign over this scandal?

McGrath: None. Or, next to none. He was informed last week, I think Thursday or Friday, that the feds were closing in on him. And as soon as the word came out at lunchtime on Monday that the governor of New York—this high-minded, somewhat self-righteous man, you know, former prosecutor, who was going to, you know, lead by example—as soon as the word came out that this man was engulfed in a prostitution sting, it wasn't "will he resign?" It was "when will he resign?"

Hawtin: But why didn't he resign on Monday?

McGrath: Ah, well . . . one scenario is that he's . . . basically, this involves a federal investigation. I mean, while it involves sex and high-priced prostitutes, it's actually about legally something more serious. It involves, you know, money and transferring money and some federal statutes. So, he, Eliot Spitzer, you know, the guy who, who cut his teeth as a prosecutor, he is now being prosecuted, and he's being prosecuted by people from the federal Justice Department. He's a Democrat, they're Republicans, and I think he's trying to cut a deal, apparently, and I think maybe being governor for another 48 hours in his mind may have given him some leverage to try to negotiate a deal.

Hawtin: So what are you hearing, though, about whether he's been able to get any concessions?

McGrath: Well, the federal prosecutor involved says no deal has been made. I mean, you can take that for what it is. You know, federal prosecutors are like anybody else . . . they can say one thing and do another, but he is not a person who invites prosecutorial mercy at this point. Ahmm . . . Getting back to what you said before, the other thing is, there were a few people that wanted him to hang on. One of them most notably was his wife, Silda Wall Spitzer. There is some speculation, though, that perhaps she didn't know the whole story. And again, this is more than possibly bad judgment and going down to Washington and carrying on with a high-priced prostitute. This involves, you know, federal money-laundering laws. In fact, this involves the very laws that Spitzer enforced when he was attorney general here in New York State, when he came down very hard on Wall Street.

Hawtin: OK, so if they do go after him full-force, what kind of charges would he be likely to face?

McGrath: I think the law is called "structuring." It's pretty serious. I think at the high end, it could be as much as, you know, 20 years in jail. That's the, you know, absolutely worst-case scenario. No one expects him to face jail time. I think the speculation is, though, that he's going to have to plead guilty, and plead guilty to a felony. When you do that, not only is it humiliating and disgraceful, but if you're Eliot Spitzer and you went to Harvard Law School, and you used to make your money as a lawyer, that's very problematic. He would lose his law license. And I think he may be negotiating with the feds on just how long he would have to be on probation, you know . . . there could be fines. It's helpful to keep in mind that Eliot Spitzer is the son of Bernard Spitzer, a self-made zillionaire. Eliot Spitzer has a lot of money at his disposal, and federal prosecutors are very aware of that. I think he could be looking at them to want him to pay a very stiff fine.

Hawtin: Well, that could explain how he could spend almost half of his after-tax income on prostitution, if it's true that he spent 80 grand. But structuring—what is that? Is that something like money laundering?

McGrath: It involves moving money from one account to another, and those laws have gotten tougher in this country ever since September 11. Basically, it involves being very fast and very loose and not very ethical with one's money.

Hawtin: But a lot of people are going to be watching whether he might get charged with being a client of a prostitute, because he was the key player in changing the prostitution laws.

McGrath: Right, yeah, although that's . . . merely being the client of a prosecutor . . . I mean, I'm sorry . . . (laughter) . . . merely being the client of a *prostitute* is a misdemeanor. On the prostitution front, more troublesome for the now-former governor is the Mann Act. And because this woman—who goes under the trade name Kristen—because Kristen was brought from New York City to Washington, and thus crossed state lines, that's a violation of the 100-year-old federal law called the Mann Act. Indeed, Mr. Spitzer could be prosecuted for violating the Mann Act, but giving every . . . everything else that this crazy case involves, that's almost the least of his troubles.

Hawtin: You don't think he's going to go to jail, though?

McGrath: No. I, no, I don't think he'll go to jail. I mean, he might go to metaphorical jail; he'll be reduced to nothing. He already said this morning, when he resigned, he's done in public life, he's done in politics, he wants to make some kind of contribution, but you know, he's been humiliated, disgraced. I mean, you know, he's, he's not going to be confined in the federal prison system, which is a pretty horrible place in America, but his life has taken an amazing tumble in a couple of days.

Hawtin: But you know, a lot of people thought that he was going to be the politician who was going to bring about some really important changes in New York.

McGrath: Oh, absolutely, and New York State needs important changes. The state government here is corrupt, it's dysfunctional, it's inefficient. The economy in New York State is not good. What we call upstate New York, which is basically anything beyond New York, or New York City, the economy has struggled for a long time. And, and people did indeed think that things were going to change; people were very hopeful. Ah, Spitzer was elected in November of 2006 with 69 point something percent of the vote. It was a record landslide. And Spitzer leaves an enormous burden for a nonetheless very capable fellow named David Paterson, who was his lieutenant governor and as of Monday will, will be the new governor.

Hawtin: So you think that the reforms that he was working on, they won't be lost? That they'll be picked up?

McGrath: One would hope. Ah, one of the points I'm making in an editorial for tomorrow is that, is the status quo in New York is very powerful. Nineteen million people in New York State are, are ill-served by what's really a bad government. But there's a small handful of people that profit from that very government. And you know, that status quo is not gonna want to change. But the people in the legislature, the people that despised Eliot Spitzer, they now have one less reason to oppose these reforms now.

Hawtin: OK, Jim, and thanks very much for talking to us.

McGrath: Sure.

Hawtin: Jim McGrath is the chief editorial writer for the Albany *Times Union*, and we reached him, as you might expect, in Albany.

It's Senator Clinton

Times Union editorial, November 8, 2000

New York's next senator is Hillary Rodham Clinton—who was raised in Illinois, educated in Massachusetts and Connecticut, and came into politics in Arkansas and Washington. Her triumph on Tuesday, as a New Yorker now in her own right, ensures this much of an extension of a Clinton legacy.

Mrs. Clinton's challenge now is to bring to her office the success of government during the Clinton years without the distractions and accompanying political warfare. New York, especially upstate, needs a senator committed to spreading the riches of a transformed and still vibrant economy. She'd do well to follow the example of her colleague, Senator Charles Schumer, in that regard. Her burden is to deliver on the 200,000 upstate jobs she has pledged to help create.

How successful she is as a senator will depend, to a large extent, on whether she can steer clear of the narrow, partisan, and potentially ugly atmosphere that's likely to dominate the next Congress. Mrs. Clinton is an accomplished crusader, but also a scarred one, on her party's and on the administration's behalf. It's up to her to demonstrate a willingness to work with both the Senate's majority and its minority.

If ever there was the occasion for shedding her image as one who regards the political opposition as the enemy army, this is it.

Mrs. Clinton's campaign was remarkable for its demonstrated ability to get the voters in a large, diverse, and once rather foreign state to see her quite differently from an image of her that developed over eight years as First Lady. American politics does indeed allow for such sea changes.

Mrs. Clinton needs to seize another chance to break with the politics of the past by pushing for campaign finance reform legislation—above all else—when she takes office in January. Her race against Representative Rick Lazio was marked, among other things, by notable progress toward restricting the influence of the unregulated funds known as "soft money." The candidate's motives may have been suspect, and the execution was rather haphazard. But the issue resonated with the voters.

The story nationally was altogether different. Soft money obscures the excessive amounts of legal, hard money. The presidential and congressional elections cost, all counted, about $3 billion. Mrs. Clinton says her race has made her a zealot for campaign finance reform. Well, time to get it done. That means publicly financed campaigns, not campaigns run on special-interest money.

In just two months, it'll be Mrs. Clinton, not her husband, who occupies a high position in Washington. If only her Washington is a more liberated and responsive place than his was.

NATIONAL

Farewell, Mister Speaker

Times Union opinion piece, January 9, 1994

Times changed, but Tip O'Neill's politics didn't

There was a time, back in the early Reagan years, back when the safety net was sagging and few people seemed to care, that it was quite politically fashionable to say that New Deal politics were dead. Only it wasn't quite true. At least one person continued to fight for the poor and the disenfranchised, and against the budget-cutters and the glorification of the rich.

He was Tip O'Neill. He was the leading Democrat in the country at that point, and he wasn't about to waver after a lifetime commitment to economic justice just because of the Reagan crowd, and because the writers on pages like this said his politics were obsolete. With his death the other day at 81, an era really has ended in American politics. Oh, liberalism managed to survive for the most part, and the Democrats are even back in power. But never again will someone the likes of Tip O'Neill occupy such a prominent place in American politics.

He was born in Cambridge, Massachusetts, in the part of town where, as Jimmy Breslin liked to point out, the people didn't go to Harvard.

"At the age of 14 I landed a summer job as a groundskeeper, cutting the grass and trimming the hedges at Harvard. It was tough work, and I was paid 17 cents an hour," O'Neill writes in his memoirs, *Man of the House.*

"On a beautiful June day, as I was going about my daily grind, the class of 1927 gathered in a huge tent to celebrate commencement. Inside, I could see hundreds of young men standing around in their white linen suits, laughing and talking. . . . as I watched those privileged, confident Ivy League Yankees who had everything handed to them in life, I made a resolution. Someday, I vowed, I would work to make sure my own people could go to places like Harvard."

O'Neill was one of the boys from Barry's Corner. He went to college at night, and lost his first try for office, for the Cambridge City Council, by about 150 votes because he hadn't quite learned the art of campaigning. He merely assumed that his neighbor, a Mrs. O'Brien, would vote for him because he shoveled her walk and mowed her lawn. He hadn't learned, yet, that he had to ask for her vote, and everyone else's. Sometimes he had to do more than ask; he had to lobby, he had to pressure people, and mostly, he had to count—like he did during the impeachment proceedings against Richard Nixon and when he led the mostly successful fight against aid to the contras in Nicaragua.

He took John Kennedy's congressional seat in 1953, but few outside of Massachusetts had much reason to notice him until about 1973 or 1974. He was the House majority leader then, and the one who steered the impeachment proceedings through the House. Breslin tells the story in one of the great books about modern American politics, *How the Good Guys Finally Won*, a tale of triumph of men like O'Neill, Peter Rodino, and Judge John Sirica.

When Nixon was finished, and the presidency was in the hands of Gerald Ford, a Republican, yes, still a pal of O'Neill's from the House, O'Neill recalled a conversation: "Jerry, isn't this a wonderful country? Here we can talk like this and be friends, and eighteen months from now, I'll be going around the country kicking your ass in."

· Two administrations later, it did look for a time like he might be through. The Republicans tried to prop him up as a symbol of everything wrong with American government, and a bunch of younger, less principled, and more image-conscious people in his own party thought his time had come and gone. But look who prevailed.

O'Neill had no reason to be image conscious. He liked to drink—everyone knew that—and was practically a cartoon parody of himself. During his early days as Speaker of the House, *Saturday Night Live* did a wonderful skit on a State of the Union address, complete with John Belushi as Tip O'Neill, sitting in the big chair and stuffing his face.

He was also, I think, about as genuine and sincere as anyone in politics. He saw it, or most of it, from the other side. His dig at Lyndon B. Johnson was that "if you had four stars on your shoulder, he believed everything you said." He came out against the Vietnam War after talking with kids, his own as well as those on the campuses. His staunch opposition to US military involvement in Latin America, on the other hand, was said to have been influenced at least in part by a cousin who was a Maryknoll nun in Latin America, and who held similar views herself.

Just look at who's in Congress now. Look at the slick people in leadership jobs who go on the Sunday morning TV shows and talk in sound bites. What do they really stand for?

Now we have guys in Congress like Bob Packwood, who no longer even lives in the state he's supposed to represent, and who can't even go back without storming out of news conferences after just a few tough but legitimate questions about his record and his behavior. And then think about Tip O'Neill, who never really changed, from the day he was elected to the Massachusetts legislature in 1936 to his retirement from Congress in 1986.

"I'm still a bread-and-butter Democrat who believes that every family deserves the opportunity to own a home, educate their children and afford medical care," he said in his memoirs. "This is the American dream, and it's still worth fighting for. In my view, the federal government has an obligation to help you along the line until you reach that dream. And when you do, you have an obligation to help out the next group that comes along."

Perhaps we've reached the point where that sounds sappy, and as unrealistic as anything Ronald Reagan ever told us. But for 50 years, as he learned to ask voters for their support, they were glad to have him back. Just ask anyone from the Eighth Congressional District in Massachusetts.

His body lies in state today at the State House in Boston, and they're mourning back in Cambridge, from Barry's Corner to Harvard Yard, and over to MIT and the futuristic scene. In a city where cultures clash daily, he'll be remembered as he should be: as a statesman from the rough and tumble school.

Some Names Worth Hearing Once Again

Times Union opinion piece, November 16, 2002

Now the name-calling begins. The Republicans aren't content with licking their chops in the delight that perhaps the Democrats have miscalculated with their choice of Representative Nancy Pelosi of California as their leader in the House of Representatives.

She comes from the progressive wing of her party, certainly. And she represents San Francisco. Dust off the label, then. Cue up the sound bite. Pelosi is a . . . "San Francisco Democrat."

It's been 18 years since that phrase was introduced. Jeane Kirkpatrick had used it, over and over, in a rather ugly speech to the 1984 GOP convention in Dallas.

The Republicans were there to nominate Ronald Reagan for a second term, the one that flirted with fiscal and foreign policy disaster. Kirkpatrick's errand that August was to counterattack the Democrats, for what they had said and done at their own convention the prior month in, where else, San Francisco.

What an image. San Francisco and the Democrats gathered there, embodied in the harsh eyes of partisan opposition. The Left Coast, hippies, feminism in full force, and, of course, drugs, gays, and a relatively new disease known as AIDS. "San Francisco Democrats," uttered in the right tone and context, could be quite a battle cry. Which is why the GOP is testing such retro political dialogue against Pelosi.

But what was the Democratic convention that year all about? Gary Hart had been there, in a last-ditch stand for a presidential candidacy that urged his party to rethink New Deal and Great Society politics and break free of such traditional constituencies as organized labor. Jesse Jackson had made a heartfelt speech, apologizing for his then quite infamous "Hymietown" slur and aiming for a higher ground as he abandoned his improbable presidential quest. The nominee, Walter Mondale—yes, that Walter Mondale—was frank enough to say that the Reagan era deficits required a tax increase. He was right, of course.

And then there was the speech. Mario M. Cuomo, still in his first term as governor, electrified the convention and the TV audience watching it. His theme was, imagine, the gap between rich and poor that the Republicans didn't seem to see or understand. That speech is still well worth quoting.

> A shining city is perhaps all the president sees from the portico of the White House and the veranda of his ranch, where everyone seems to be doing well.
>
> There's another part to the shining city; the part where some people can't pay their mortgages, and most young people can't

afford one; where students can't afford the education they need, and middle-class parents watch the dreams they hold for their children evaporate.

In this part of the city there are more poor than ever, more families in trouble, more and more people who need help but can't find it. . . .

And there are people who sleep in the city streets, in the gutter, where the glitter doesn't show.

There are ghettos where thousands of young people, without a job or an education, give their lives away to drug dealers every day.

There is despair, Mr. President, in the faces that you don't see, in the places that you don't visit in your shining city.

In fact, Mr. President . . . this nation is more a "Tale of Two Cities" than it is just a "Shining City on a Hill."

Two years into the Bush administration, so similar in so many ways to the early years of the Reagan administration, Pelosi can look forward to being called a "San Francisco Democrat."

The others in her party can expect to hear that, too.

Their response should be so simple:

"'San Francisco Democrat?' What's wrong with that?"

INTERNATIONAL

A Chance for Peace in Ulster

Times Union editorial, May 22, 1997

The latest attempt to end the ages of madness in Northern Ireland comes, this time, from across the sea in London. Prime Minister Tony Blair's government, in power less than a month, is talking already with Sinn Fein, the political arm of the Irish Republican Army.

That is as welcome a change in British policy as it is an essential opportunity for the Sinn Fein/IRA movement to end its ways of terror. Mr. Blair's speed in making his overture to Sinn Fein also drives home the point of how urgent it is to save a stalled peace process from dying.

The last time there was this much reason for hope was almost three years ago, when it was initiated from the other side. For the first time in a generation, the IRA bombings stopped. The IRA held to a cease-fire for 17 months, but Sinn Fein and the British were unable to make any diplomatic progress that remotely matched the opportunities that the cease-fire presented.

The prime minister in London then was John Major, whom Mr. Blair defeated handily in the May 1 elections. Under Mr. Major, there were always more promises that needed to be made and verified, new conditions that needed to be met before Sinn Fein could be welcomed as a partner in a serious dialogue about peace. Mr. Major had a way of shifting the focus onto issues that should have been secondary, like how the IRA would disarm itself.

Such distractions are over, for now. By approaching Sinn Fein, and by letting two high-profile IRA prisoners serve out their sentences in Ulster rather than England, Mr. Blair can credibly ask if the IRA is ready to stick to politics and not violence. "If they are, I will not be slow in my response," he says. "If they are not, they can expect no sympathy or understanding."

Not everything in Britain, then, has changed. Mr. Blair's expectation now is, not at all unreasonably, an absence of the very IRA attacks that disrupted England during the spring election campaign. The condition for Sinn Fein's much-needed inclusion in formal peace talks is another cease-fire.

The next move must come from Belfast. John Hume, a leader of the Catholic mainstream who has worked with Sinn Fein but is hardly above criticizing it, is quite blunt. He says Sinn Fein should seize this opportunity, which it might not have again for who knows how long.

In the heady days of early 1995, in the midst of the last cease-fire and not long before President Clinton's triumphant visit to Belfast, Sinn Fein leader Gerry Adams made a triumphant visit of his own to the United States. In a speech at the Hibernian Hall in Albany, Mr. Adams spoke of the then rather bright prospects for better times in Northern Ireland. "Let our revenge be in the laughter of our children," he said.

That still should be the goal. But now this generation, Mr. Adams especially, must act in the interests of the next.

Mr. Adams and Mr. Blair

Times Union editorial, December 20, 1997

What a picture it made, Gerry Adams beaming outside the British prime minister's residence. Not since Michael Collins was let into 10 Downing Street in 1921 had a leader of Sinn Fein been received this way. That meeting made permanent the separation of the Irish Republic and Northern Ireland, and might very well have led to Mr. Collins's assassination.

The British government can try, as it has, to play down the significance of the meeting between Mr. Adams and Prime Minister Tony Blair. No matter. This was history. In time, their meeting might stand out as a moment when all of Ireland got past the Troubles and embraced an era of peace.

Or it might stand out, just as starkly, as another symbol of the peace that a land so torn by violence could have had, but rejected. But it stands, already, as a gauge of how far the hopes for Irish peace have advanced. It wasn't long ago that it was illegal in Britain to so much as broadcast Mr. Adams's voice.

History, though, is as much about opportunity as it is about progress. That's especially true when the relevant history is so full of the casualties of lost opportunity. Since 1969, the history of Northern Ireland and Britain is best measured by the 3,200 lives that have been lost.

That's what motivated Mr. Blair and Mr. Adams to meet, and that's how each of them can defend doing so to their respective detractors.

When the pleasantries were over in London last week, and Mr. Adams had bid "Happy Christmas" to the crowd at No. 10, the most enduring words were Mr. Blair's warning against more of the violence that was raging just earlier this year. To resume the bombings, he said, would be to "waste the best possibility for peace that we have had in a generation."

So now what? Isn't it time for David Trimble, the Ulster Unionist Party leader, to do as Mr. Blair has done? Only now the history that's been made clashes with all the obstacles that the present still poses. The Unionists will have none of it, of course. Bad enough, to them, that Mr. Blair would do something that's as necessary as it is bold.

"And where's the next step?" Ken Maginnis, an Ulster Unionist Party spokesman, asked in a sneering tone. "Adams and Trimble and Blair walking arm and arm . . . then being required to dance a jig?"

OK, so no jigs just yet. The spirit of the cease-fire and the ongoing peace talks will do for now. In time, Mr. Trimble might see it Mr. Adams's way, as Adams put it in a visit to Albany almost three years ago. "Let our revenge be in the laughter of our children," he said that night in March of 1995.

What pictures those would be, of an Ireland at peace.

Ireland's Peace Must Prevail

Times Union editorial, August 20, 1998

In the lush but haunted land of Ireland, not even a historic peace accord can halt the miserable act of burying the innocent victims of unyielding hatred. And so Tuesday in the tiny northern Irish village of Augher had a priest from the Catholic parish praying that the savage car bombing in the nearby town of Omagh might mark the end of 30 years of unrelenting civil war.

The Reverend James Grimes spoke of the great faith of Avril Monaghan, who was 30 years old and pregnant with twins when she was killed along with her 18-month-old daughter. There are 26 more victims, Catholic and Protestant alike, to pray for similarly. Is faith tested so severely anywhere else?

It was just a month ago that there was reason to hope that perhaps Northern Ireland had come to confront, in all its collective outrage, a turning point. The deaths of three young brothers, from a household and family of both religions, in a firebombing committed by Protestant terrorists had so many people aghast at the sheer magnitude of a new standard of horror in their midst.

But the defectors from the Irish Republican Army are not to be deterred. The so-called Real IRA is a movement that claims, by best estimates, barely 100 people. It insists on continuing the very war that the IRA itself and its political allies in the Sinn Fein Party wisely have abandoned.

The Real IRA's explanation for its terrorism is an unspeakably cynical one. To claim the real target was a commercial one and that the deaths of civilians were unintended is revolting. Its attempt to apologize for the carnage it has wrought is obscene. To declare now that such violence will stop merely underscores the ugly and irreversible damage this group already has done.

Sinn Fein leader Gerry Adams has denounced the Omagh attack in the strongest of terms. A nationalist hard-liner who has embraced and savored the victory of an arduous peace process knows perhaps better than anyone that there can be no turning back in Ireland. It is encouraging that the commitment to peace that is shared among Belfast, Dublin, and London extends to a determination to crush the last bastion of pro-nationalist terrorism. But it is crucial that any crackdown on the Real IRA and any other enemies of peace not violate the sense and spirit of democracy that prevails, even still, in the wake of the ratification of the Good Friday accord. That means no imprisonment without trial, even for suspected terrorists. It means never losing sight of all that has been won this year, despite two of the most heinous instances of deadly violence in recent Irish history.

Such is the burden of Ireland's test of resolve and faith.

George Mitchell, Peacemaker

Times Union editorial, October 22, 1998

George Mitchell has a way of making it so much easier to understand just how decades of sectarian bloodshed in Ireland gave way to a historic if still tenuous peace accord. The two years of negotiations that he mediated stand out as the triumph of hope and perseverance. Violence can't stop Northern Ireland from entering a new era. Neither can still unresolved matters of contention like the decommissioning of the weapons that prevailed before the votes did. To return to a haunted and deadly past is unacceptable. So the Irish will find their way.

Mr. Mitchell was the gentle but determined force that kept the arduous and often bitter peace talks from collapsing. For that, many felt he deserved at least part of the Nobel Peace Prize, which instead went to John Hume, leader of Northern Ireland's largest Catholic political party, and David Trimble, head of the Ulster Unionists.

Mr. Mitchell, though, has a wider view, and an unselfish one. His position is that the prize should have been shared by all eight political parties—including the Sinn Fein movement led by Gerry Adams—that took part in the peace negotiations, and by the governments in Dublin and London as well.

For consolation, there's the honorary degree and warm reception he received at the College of Saint Rose Tuesday, ever fitting for the world-renowned statesman he has become.

In a land that he thinks might actually be too aware, if that's possible, of its own history, Mr. Mitchell was the one who kept looking ahead to what the future might bring. Prospects for keeping the peace only get better as economic conditions do. The mediator saw pockets of despair in Northern Ireland, where a third of the population has never so much as held a job. And so the solution is simple: foreign trade and investment.

The other lessons offered by Mr. Mitchell are similarly easy to digest if not entirely heed. He's adamant that the Irish must not set the bar too high. Singling out conditions that could doom the further implementation of the Good Friday peace accord might well be a self-fulfilling prophecy. America has to overcome the daily violence that it cannot eliminate, and so must Ireland.

On that, his optimism shines through. Once he counted the votes as the majority leader in the US Senate. Now he sees the Irish support their peace treaty with an 85 percent majority. "The people of Ireland have spoken," Mr. Mitchell says. "The people do not want to go back to the bitterness and violence."

He will not be dissuaded.

Day of Terror

Times Union editorial, September 12, 2001

The nation proves all too vulnerable to forces intent on missions of hate

By midmorning on Tuesday, America was a different country, shaken to its core by a chilling series of unprovoked events that amounted to the conditions and circumstances of wartime.

The cloudless New York sky blew apart, setting off a day not to be forgotten. From coast to coast, normal business and the most ordinary activities were disrupted. Airline travel was halted, and in a country where it's essential. Primary elections were postponed, leaving democracy itself a temporary casualty of the horrific chain of events. Schools were closed. President Bush, on a visit to Florida at the time of the blast, was moved to the safe quarters of US military bases before returning to Washington under heavy security. Lives were changed, and lives were lost.

The actual casualty toll, no doubt into the thousands, still is left to the worst of imaginations.

This isn't supposed to happen, not in civilized environments and most certainly not within our own borders.

More to the point, it can't happen. Not again. The peculiar form of violence and hatred known as terrorism can be tolerated no more.

Government must act, of course, firmly but responsibly—and with all the resolve so frequently absent in the past.

Among the citizenry, conversely, calm is in order. Needless domestic panic does nothing to control the horror that can't be undone. For the most basic functions of daily life to resume—as President George W. Bush reminded the nation Tuesday night—is a powerful statement in its own right.

First, it must be made clear just who is responsible. Early information that seems to point to the Afghan terrorist Osama bin Laden must be developed further. Others can't yet be ruled out.

Retaliation ultimately will be as tricky as it is imperative. Punishment of the perpetrators alone would be pointless, and perhaps even counterproductive. The enemy here answers the eerie call of martyrdom.

It's neither misguided nor premature to see the world in two groups—the countries that condone terrorism and harbor terrorists against the countries that condemn it. That's the battle the United States needs to fight, and with the enlightened world every bit engaged. President Bush underscored just that point Tuesday night, saying there should be no distinction made in pursuing those engaged in the twin evils of committing acts of terrorism or harboring others who do.

There are obvious questions about the adequacy of national security that must be addressed immediately. Already there are suggestions that the Bush administration should divert money from its proposed missile defense shield to other forms of counterterrorism efforts—more intelligence gathering, for example, and a greater emphasis on monitoring and intercepting suspicious persons.

Surely, there must be a greater emphasis on battling such terrorism from within US borders. For years, there have been warnings of possible bioterrorism, for example, with countries like Iraq providing the laboratories needed to produce deadly agents that could spread doom in populated areas. That threat needs to be taken more seriously.

And there have been warning signs, very vague but very ugly, of the kind of attacks that struck New York and Washington on Tuesday. The truck bomb explosion at, yes, the World Trade Center, in 1993 was one of them. It was a wake-up call that the US mainland was not immune from terrorism. Several years ago, an informant helped foil a plot to bomb the Lincoln Tunnel—a clear sign that terrorists were a threat from within.

Another event that sprang to mind on Tuesday was the 1988 bombing of Pan Am Flight 103 over Scotland. The word went out after that December day: Lockerbie, or something like it, could happen in the United States.

If Tuesday proved anything, it's that terrorists who are determined to kill Americans will find a way to do so. Today, they lack the technology to launch rogue missile attacks. But tomorrow, who is to say they won't, especially if they feel that there is no other avenue of attack left open to them?

For the immediate future, though, critics are right to urge far greater emphasis on conventional attacks. Tuesday's strikes showed how diabolically ingenious terrorists can be.

Another huge security question is how the attackers were able to penetrate security at three different airports and hijack four passenger airlines within a short period of time. After years of beefing up airport security, it seemed as if hijackings had been relegated to an earlier era. But now, in one morning, that sense of security was shown to be deadly porous.

What comes now?

The answer lies in the raw wreckage left along the country's busiest urban corridor, from New York City to Washington, in all the unsifted intelligence reports in all those US government installations and through surveillance technology that defies even the imagination of the modern age.

Acts that constitute the immoral equivalent of war require revenge—as swift as it is sure, as unyielding as it is on target, as convincing as it is calculated. A nation that knows both success and discomfort with the politics and mechanics of warfare might brace for such distasteful measures yet again.

Editors' note: Howard Healy contributed to this editorial.

The Day After

Times Union editorial, September 13, 2001

The dawn's early light showed a country already confronting the aftermath of what President Bush rightly called an attempt to incite first fear, and then chaos, upon us.

There were bodies, by the thousands upon thousands, to recover and even some survivors to rescue. There were reassurances to be made, about the singular purpose of federal government back in session and about a global economy that won't be disrupted by an unprovoked, unprecedented, and unspeakable attack on the very nerve of the country.

But, mostly, there were war (no other word seems appropriate) plans that needed to be made. If the first order of the day was to show the fierce resolve of an undaunted nation, the next was the more difficult task of preparing to launch the appropriate force upon those behind this assault.

Mr. Bush appeared more forceful and convincing than he had been the previous night as he spoke again to a nation much in need of answers. This time, he actually said war—in a fitting characterization of what's been thrust upon the American people.

Suddenly, money is not an issue, he says, for the struggle that's now required against the forces of terrorism. Mr. Bush promised victory against such evil, but he might have added that it will be neither quick nor easy.

A country that's had such immediate successes, at least in the short term, in military missions in the Persian Gulf and Kosovo would do well to anticipate something quite different. Ensuring that a day like Tuesday never comes again will be a lengthy and complex endeavor if, indeed, it's even possible. If recent military clashes had the effect of sanitizing war, what lies ahead is almost certain to dispel those illusions.

It needs to be understood and addressed that the prior US responses against similar terrorism were inadequate. Unsustained counterattacks in retaliation for the 1998 attacks on US embassies in Kenya and Tanzania and on the *USS Cole* last year achieved little—except, perhaps, inviting more of the same.

And it needs to be reiterated that the brutal circumstances ahead are harder still because of the lack of a readily identifiable enemy. The easy targets, military as well as political, are no substitutes for the right targets.

Such are the conditions facing the United States on Day 3 of its gravest threat to national security since the Cold War. Dangers abound—of not reacting aggressively enough, and of lashing out against the wrong people and the wrong lands. Civil liberties must be guarded at home, just as the nation is set to act with absolute conviction against those responsible for this sense of siege, here and abroad.

Mr. Bush is quite untested for this, for events for which there really is no adequate preparation. He proceeds, though, with the great advantage of a nation undeterred and where the flag still stands.

Rising from the Ruins One Year Later,
A Pause to Ponder How We Have Changed

September 11, 2002

Introduction to the *Times Union*'s special section on the September 11, 2001, attacks

New York, and America, remember today what cannot be forgotten.

New York, and America, confront wounds today that haven't healed, not in a single year, and perhaps never will. They feel loss that was once beyond all but the most fatalistic of imaginations and that now is simply permanent.

The country is at war today, with no end in sight. The dead are mourned, the survivors are comforted, and the battle goes on.

So it's a solemn day this September 11, across a land where the collective patriotism shouldn't be questioned.

America's dignity and perseverance will carry this day. What's required is what Americans do so well. We know how to live and, regrettably, how to die.

Only more is required. There are still questions that have no ready answers.

Hours after the towers were hit and the first casualties were identified, it was taken on faith that this was suddenly a different country.

Is it really? If so, just how different?

A year ago, the flags went up, prayers were offered, dissent was muted, and it qualified as resilience, if not defiance, to go about daily life where the terrorists had struck the most savagely.

In Albany, state government rushed to convene on September 13. Speeches full of emotion and unusual lucidity were made in the Capitol, an unlikely place for that on less trying days.

In Washington, President Bush promised New York $20 billion, no conditions and no questions.

And then?

Government functioned, but not without all the enduring signs of the usual politics. A peek behind a flag could reveal a country that still contained an "us" and a "them."

In time, there were more casualties, not from terrorism but from the war against it.

And now?

To get a sense of that requires a careful inventory of civil liberties. The losses of a year ago we've tallied, we think. Was the Constitution among them? It requires, too, a closer-than-ever examination of national and internal security—not a reassuring exercise.

And it demands sustained commitment to a war about which not nearly enough is known. It needs a dialogue of a sort that isn't always welcome.

As it happened, the attacks of last September 11 came on what was supposed to be an election day. A sign of the unprecedented horrors of that day came when such a fundamental American exercise as voting was canceled.

A year later, the recollection of the attacks comes just one day after millions of people, in New York and elsewhere, again were able to vote. That they could is a testament to the survival of American democracy. How many of them actually did raises a tougher question about the prevalence of that democracy, still not free from the terrorist threat that writer Christopher Hitchens calls a brand of fascism.

So what's become of a city, a state, and a country—more vulnerable yet more buoyant, more resolved but still uncertain—after a year of a war against their very being?

Read on, and reflect.

Jim read a newspaper with total absorption and an editor's eye. Here, he starts a day on Cape Cod with coffee and a newspaper at a cottage he and Darryl rented in Wellfleet in 2002 and 2003 (above). On the facing page, he relaxes at outdoor cafés in Chicago on a visit to that city in October 2004, (top); and during his honeymoon there with Darryl in June 2001 (bottom) as he catches up on the headlines in a great newspaper town. Photographs by Darryl McGrath.

Jim seldom used his press pass, although he kept it within easy reach in his *Times Union* office for the rare occasions when he needed press credentials. Like all good journalists, he often thought about his next topic, even in his off time. He instinctively gathered tips, developed sources, and tapped into the mood of the city by getting out of the newsroom and into the places so many of his editorials described: barrooms; outdoor festivals; city parks; the less-traveled neighborhoods and back streets, on his bike; campaign headquarters on primary night; and the state Capitol for the spontaneous celebrations that unfolded the night that New York passed its marriage equality law. Photograph courtesy of the *Times Union*.

Dear Jim,

We have had some run! We did many good things at HUD. I thank you for the time, professionalism and thoughtful presentation. There is so much we can — and should do.

To the future ...

Sincerely,
Andrew

ANDREW CUOMO
THE SECRETARY OF HOUSING AND URBAN DEVELOPMENT

Jim's readership included the famous and the infamous. Jim had kept these two notes in his desk, where they were found after his death. New York Governor Andrew Cuomo wrote to Jim as his tenure as US Secretary of Housing and Urban Development in the Clinton administration drew to a close and he prepared to return to New York, where he planned to continue his political career. With notes like this, Cuomo laid the groundwork for friendly relationships with people and institutions whose good graces he would need in upcoming campaigns. Cuomo maintained regular and

> 2/12/98
>
> Your editorial on Thursday (2/12) brushed subttely on a far deeper issue, regarding the shrinking welfare rolls. In particular the rise in inmate populations on both county and state levels.
>
> Some say screw the humilation at welfare and resort to crime. Let's face it, MacDonald's can't support a home.
>
> The Bloods
> 031

warm contact with Jim for years, especially so through a difficult period for Cuomo after his marriage to Kerry Kennedy ended and he dropped his Democratic primary bid for the governor's race in 2002. Cuomo's calls to Jim became less frequent during his tenure as New York's attorney general and had ceased by the time Cuomo was elected governor in 2010. The note from the gang member was written on a piece of cardboard torn from a box and was signed "The Bloods 031." The otherwise unidentified author of this note praised an editorial Jim had written about welfare in 2010.

Jim wrote a 2002 Memorial Day tribute to the first Capital Region soldier to die in the War in Afghanistan by spending a day in the tiny Berkshire town where US Army Sergeant First Class Daniel Petithory grew up and was buried (see page 143). This photo shows Sergeant Petithory's grave in Cheshire, Massachusetts, which his friends had decorated with symbols of his life. Jim was a voracious reader and natural conversationalist who often summoned a literary reference to accompany his writing—for this piece, Carl Sandburg's poem "Grass"—and always spoke to people he encountered along the way as he developed an editorial or op-ed. The op-ed he wrote about that day reflects both attributes. Photograph by Darryl McGrath.

Dear Editor,   2/22/06

    I read your editorial about my case on February 15, 2006. I wanted to say thank you and that I appreciate your opinions.

    What you wrote is very true. DeAngelis used threats of extreme amounts of time to have me plead guilty to an amount of time I don't deserve. Her original plea bargain offer was forty-five years. Knowing this made me believe I would easily get fifty to seventy-five years if I lost trial.

    All I can do now is try for the appeal and make the best of my time in prison. In June of 2005 I received my G.E.D., and now I am working on an Associate's Degree. I am also a teacher's aide for the high school class to help others get their G.E.D.

    So thank you, and know my family, friends and I all appreciate your editorials.

Jon Romano

Jon Romano
DIN # 05-A-0010

Jim kept many of the letters he received from readers, some of whom had been directly affected by his editorials. This poignant letter is from Jon Romano, who was convicted of firing a gun in a Capital Region high school as a teenager, accepted a harsh plea deal against the advice of his attorney, and unsuccessfully tried to appeal his conviction. The *Times Union* editorial board took a compassionate view of this troubled young man's plight in an editorial written by Jim (see page 94).

September 12, 2013

Mrs. Darryl McGrath
Trinity United Methodist Church
235 Lark St.
Albany, NY 12210

Dear Mrs. McGrath,

On behalf of everyone here at the Boston Red Sox, please accept my deepest condolences on your husband's tragic passing.

Jim was an exemplary member of Red Sox Nation who made us proud with his willingness to fly the flag deep behind enemy lines. We're continually grateful for those who carry their love of our team from Boston to other locations, especially those in less hospitable outposts. From what I've heard, Jim was also a consummate journalist who exuded a passion for his craft and a commitment to his community, and he leaves behind a tremendous legacy.

Please know that we're thinking of you and your family, and we will always be obliged to your husband for his dedication and decency.

Sincerely,

Larry Lucchino

This condolence letter to Darryl from Larry Lucchino, the president and chief executive officer of the Boston Red Sox, arrived at the Trinity United Methodist Church in Albany September 14, 2013, where Jim's memorial service took place later that day. Jim grew up in the Brighton section of Boston, close to Fenway Park, the home field of the Red Sox, and he remained an avid Red Sox fan for the rest of his life. The letter arrived in an express delivery envelope with no indication of who had arranged for it to be sent. It was not until June 2016 that Darryl learned that the letter had been requested by Jim's friend and fellow Red Sox fan Wanda Fischer, Albany's renowned expert on Appalachian-influenced folk music and long-time host of the WAMC FM radio program *Hudson River Sampler*.

THE WHITE HOUSE
WASHINGTON

September 24, 2013

Ms. Darryl McGrath
6 Irving Street
Albany, New York 12202

Dear Darryl:

I was saddened to hear about the passing of your husband, Jim McGrath. Please accept my sympathies as you mourn his loss and reflect upon his life.

My thoughts and prayers are with you. I hope you will be consoled by the memories of your time with Jim and comforted by the presence of family and friends.

Sincerely,

Jim never met Barack Obama, and Darryl never learned how the president was informed of Jim's death.

UNITED STATES SENATE
WASHINGTON, D.C. 20510

September, 2013

Dear Editorial Board members,

I wanted to send a note to offer my sincere condolences on the passing of your great colleague, Jim McGrath. I know that he was loved and respected by his colleagues, and I shared that deep respect.

I read Steve Barnes's obituary feature and thought he said it perfectly – so many of his descriptions brought back vivid memories of my interactions with Jim. Several times over the years, Jim engaged me in debate when I visited the Board. Usually he was pushing me to embrace a more progressive position, and I would have to respond with why that wasn't pragmatic given the current state of the Congress, all the while appreciating the intelligence and passion of his position. Most years as I marched down Washington Avenue in the St. Patrick's Day Parade, I would spot his beard and Red Sox jacket in the crowd by Capitol Park and yell greetings to him from my builhorn. Even there, he'd slip something in about where I should be on the big national issue of the day.

Certainly I didn't know him the way you all did, but I will miss him and his work just the same. To you, who lost not only a valued colleague but a friend, I offer you my prayers and sincere wish that his legacy of diligence, passion, commitment to improving the lives of others and professional excellence continues to inspire your work.

Sincerely,

Chuck Schumer

US Senator Charles Schumer and Jim enjoyed many an exchange over the years in *Times Union* editorial board meetings. Senator Schumer sent this warm and deeply personal letter to the *Times Union* after Jim's death.

New Yorkers for
A(ternatives
to the Death Penalty

Honors
David Kaczynski
on his Retirement as Executive Director

April 22, 2013
Albany, New York

SOCIAL JUSTICE

David Kaczynski, the brother of Unabomber Theodore Kaczynski, lived in the Capital Region when he made the unimaginably difficult decision to inform the FBI of his brother's whereabouts in Montana. Jim wrote several editorials that lauded David Kaczynski's decision and castigated the federal government for its initial decision to seek the death penalty in the Unabomber case. Theodore Kaczynski instead received a sentence of life in prison. David and Jim remained friends for the rest of Jim's life, and Jim considered David Kaczynski an enduring example of moral courage that he cited years later in his op-ed "Boston, the Bulgers, and Me," which ran in the *Times Union* in August 2013, just before Jim's death. The op-ed contrasted David Kaczynski's laudable actions with those of the Massachusetts politician William Bulger, who was long suspected of knowing the whereabouts of his mobster brother, Whitey Bulger, but who refused to cooperate in the search for him (see page 152). Jim wrote the piece shortly after authorities finally arrested Whitey Bulger in California and returned him to Massachusetts for a federal trial that resulted in Whitey Bulger receiving two life sentences for 11 murders.

Introduction

A Certain Faith in Humanity

Bill Federman

It's rare to find someone whose unbounded empathy and depth of feeling are matched by an ability to consistently express his views in forceful yet elegant writing. Jim McGrath was such a man. As you will read in the following selections, Jim's dedication to the pursuit of social justice in his role as chief editorial writer for the Albany *Times Union* led him to champion a wide range of victims—victims of poverty, intolerance, malice, misfortune, impersonal and wrong-headed government policies, and even of their own inner demons; in short, anyone who Jim believed had received a raw deal and deserved support and understanding. He knew that, for myriad reasons, life doesn't always proceed as planned, and he believed that hope, at the very least, should be offered to the less fortunate among us.

Jim in some ways had a rough upbringing, but in the all-too-brief time when I was lucky enough to be his friend, he was at peace with himself and his life, which, I believe, made him that much more eager to be a voice for those whose lives were in turmoil. His bully pulpit allowed him to scold, cajole, persuade, and from time to time school (but not harangue) those who had the power to right the things Jim perceived as wrong. To his great credit, he didn't understand why the human condition seems to include acceptance of institutional as well as individual cruelty or why they are tolerated and often encouraged. It was his mission, one that he wholeheartedly embraced, to expose these injustices and to propose solutions that he then did his best to see put into effect.

A life spent working for newspapers is a surefire antidote for unbridled optimism and helped make Jim a realist who knew that many of the things he railed against would never change. But this sobering knowledge didn't mean that he felt the daily battles he waged through his editorials weren't worth fighting. Indeed, justice doesn't always triumph, but carrying on the struggle to achieve it is a kind of victory in itself, and Jim found the skirmishing invigorating. In addition to issues such as gay rights, the death penalty, and misguided judicial decisions, he often wrote about the scourge of homelessness because that is the dead end to which so many paths lead. He recognized, sadly, that even though homelessness is a tragedy that, in a better world, wouldn't be tolerated, it "doesn't go away. Never has, and never will." But he kept hammering away, exposing its preventable causes and lamenting the devastation it wrought, which, rather than being a symptom of blindness to a lost cause, was a measure of his devotion to doing the right thing for its own sake. He knew no other way.

Doing the right thing can be a Sisyphean task, and it takes confidence in oneself, along with a certain faith in humanity, to persevere. Jim had both and he also had the strength to keep rolling that editorial boulder uphill each day, hoping to every so often push it over the top. As he said to me, in one way or another, about various situations: Don't let the bastards wear you down. Thankfully, Jim didn't. He could take it as well as he could dish it out and be ready, when he was most needed, for more.

Jim McGrath's world was one in which justice prevailed, with a little help from its friends. Given the choice, I think most of us would choose to live in Jim's world. I know I would.

Bill Federman has been an editor and writer since 1977 in the United States and Europe with the *Wall Street Journal*, the *Boston Globe*, and small daily newspapers in New England and New York.

More Unabomber Injustice

Times Union editorial, May 18, 1997

We'll be upfront about it. As a newspaper that so strongly opposes the death penalty, we just can't imagine what would be a good case for it. But neither can we imagine a worse case for seeking capital punishment than the Justice Department's determination to use it against Theodore Kaczynski, the Unabomber suspect.

First, there are the moral dimensions of Attorney General Janet Reno's decision. Ms. Reno, who personally opposes capital punishment, is especially well aware of the compelling case against it.

The practical concerns are even more daunting. There is absolutely no evidence to suggest that the prospect of facing the ultimate punishment was any deterrent to the Unabomber's calculated spree of 26 bombings that killed three people over 18 years. There is, though, quite powerful evidence that the death penalty had been a potential deterrent to the government even having a case to try in those bombings.

The hunt for the Unabomber was a long and particularly futile one. The government didn't even have its best lead until 1995, when the Unabomber manifesto, a 35,000-word attack against the inhumanity of industrial society, was published in the *New York Times* and the *Washington Post*. David Kaczynski, Theodore's brother, saw some haunting similarities between it and some of his brother's papers that he happened to stumble upon.

David Kaczynski, then living in Schenectady and working as a social worker, approached federal agents after months of personal anguish. He was motivated, ultimately, both by a desire to stop the bombings and the hope of saving his brother. He wanted justice, not capital punishment.

The chilling effect is now immeasurable. Anthony Biscegile, the lawyer who has represented David Kaczynski all along in his dealings with the authorities, is quite blunt and quite right that Theodore Kaczynski would not now be in custody and ready to stand trial were it not for his brother coming forward to turn him in.

David Kaczynski himself has been quite blunt and is quite right that executing his brother—whom he portrays, all genius aside, as mentally disturbed since childhood—will keep others from notifying the authorities about a loved one they suspect of such criminal activity, heinous as it might be.

The government's argument for going ahead with a capital case is that Theodore Kaczynski intentionally killed his victims, lacks remorse for doing so, is unlikely to be rehabilitated, and thus remains a danger to himself and others. Even if all that is proved to be true, it's nothing that life in prison without any chance of parole can't properly punish.

There is, too, the possibility that the government is saying it wants the death penalty but really wants Mr. Kaczynski to plead guilty, face a lesser penalty, and avoid having a trial at all. That would be especially cynical. The government's case, thanks largely to Theodore Kaczynski's own writings, appears to be a strong one. Put him on trial. But there's no need for such games.

With Theodore Kaczynski in jail, and David Kaczynski and their mother, Wanda, said to be devastated by the latest turn of events, the case is best summed up now by Mr. Biscegile. "There's no happy ending," he says. "There's a sad ending, and there's a horrific ending. What we're trying to do is avoid the horrific."

The execution of Mr. Kaczynski would indeed be horrific to his family.

As for Ms. Reno, she has recommended seeking the death penalty in 58 of more than 120 similar cases during her tenure as attorney general. By pursuing that course this time, though, she might not even have that option again. The legacy of the pursuit of such justice might well be to prevent true justice.

Editors' note: In January 1998, Theodore Kaczynski avoided trial with a guilty plea to all charges. He was sentenced to life in federal prison without the possibility of parole. He later unsuccessfully tried to withdraw his guilty plea. He is an inmate at a high-security federal prison in Colorado and has refused to see any members of his family or allow any information about him to be provided to his family. His mother, Wanda, has since died. David Kaczynski became executive director of New Yorkers Against the Death Penalty, which later changed its name to New Yorkers for Alternatives to the Death Penalty and expanded its focus to healing and reconciliation for families affected by capital crimes, as well as continued work at an international level to abolish capital punishment. David Kaczynski had become internationally renowned as a humanitarian and eloquent spokesperson against capital punishment before retiring from the organization in 2013. He and his wife, Linda Patrik, a former philosophy professor at Union College, were converts to Buddhism and worked at a Buddhist monastery in Woodstock for two years after David's retirement as executive director and operations manager, respectively. David Kaczynski got to know Jim well through Jim's writing about the Unabomber case, and in April 2011, David and Jim gave a well-attended presentation to University at Albany journalism students about the ethics and challenges of the coverage of the Unabomber case. David later honored his friendship with Jim by attending Jim's memorial service.

Cold Weather, Cold Truths

Times Union editorial, September 28, 1997

Summer is past, and so is Albany's mayoral campaign. As a political matter, the plight of the city's homeless population suddenly has less urgency. But as a practical matter, the onset of winter weather brings homelessness to a near crisis level.

For the past two winters, the Homeless Action Committee has operated a shelter on Quail Street. It had 19 beds and served as housing of the last resort for the hard core of the homeless. These are people suffering from alcoholism and other afflictions that keep them out of other facilities for the homeless.

When the rhetoric turns to people with nowhere to go freezing to death, this is the population that's at risk.

It's a population that will be in even greater danger this winter because the Quail Street shelter has been ordered closed as a result of a zoning dispute. The city maintains the shelter, which operated out of a two-story house at 148 Quail, violates the immediate neighborhood's one- and two-family zoning. The operators of the shelter contend the city knew in advance of their plans for 148 Quail. The Homeless Action Committee also says that as a shelter, 148 Quail meets the minimum zoning requirement of 125 square feet for the first occupant and 75 square feet for each additional person.

If the city's logic sounds confusing, here is where the matter becomes mind-numbing. The zoning board never provided a written explanation when it rejected a special-use permit for the shelter back in July. That left the Homeless Action Committee unable to appeal the board's decision. Instead it sued the city for not publishing the decision within a mandated five-day period. The case is now before a state court.

How long—into winter, perhaps?—the dispute might drag on in court is anyone's guess. The outrage, though, is this. If City Hall can effectively close a shelter that kept 19 desperate people off the streets, and if it can put its lawyers on the case, why can't it manage to address the heart of the matter? Where are these people supposed to go?

Mayor Jennings has advocated, as part of an overall policy on homelessness, taking a survey of street people. He wants to know how many of them there are and what their needs are. That was, months ago, a study that Jennings said would take just a few weeks. Meanwhile, is there any doubt that there are enough people, down and out, who are well served by the Quail Street shelter and others like it?

Enough of the delays. Closing a homeless shelter, not to mention leaving its operators without a normal avenue of appeal, in the summer is merely annoying. Leaving it closed, in the absence of an alternative site, as winter approaches is irresponsible.

A Lesson Taught Too Late

Times Union opinion piece, July 20, 2001

The ruined life of Phil Caiozzo, all those years on the streets and in homeless shelters, ought to have this legacy. No one should die the way he did.

Caiozzo was 48 when he died last week, a few hours after suffering from convulsions first experienced in a cell at the Albany County Jail.

The police on the streets of Albany knew him well. So did the officers and judges in City Court, and the guards and the staff at the jail.

Five years ago, Caiozzo was hospitalized following the severe withdrawal that came after one of his arrests. So it also was known, then, what happens so easily to people in his stage of the brutal disease of alcoholism. A Homeless Action Committee counselor said just that in a 1996 letter about Caiozzo to City Court.

The problem is this. Police stations, courtrooms, and jail cells are the wrong places for seriously addicted people apprehended, as Caiozzo was, in the middle of their otherwise endless drinking bouts.

That much is acknowledged this week, from the higher positions of law enforcement to the community of advocates for the homeless who held a memorial service for Caiozzo in his old haunt of Washington Park Wednesday night. Enlightenment comes too late for the man who was remembered as a shrewd survivor of the streets, and as someone constantly looking after the others who lived that way.

These people will cease drinking in custody, of course—but with often traumatic results. The convulsions that Caiozzo suffered are part of a hard-core alcoholic's all-too-frequent pain. That's why there are beds in emergency detoxification wards. The procedure more commonly known as drying out requires a level of medical supervision considerably more sophisticated than a jail provides.

Most likely, Caiozzo would have been seen by a doctor at the county jail sometime on the morning of July 12. Only he was dying at Albany Medical Center Hospital by then, about 24 hours after he was arrested on charges of harassment, disorderly conduct, and trespassing.

The notion of a victimless crime may border on an oxymoron. It's three decades, and fewer deaths in holding cells and drunk tanks, since public intoxication was decriminalized in New York. What Caiozzo was charged with, taunting and threatening customers at a convenience store and disrupting traffic on an adjacent street, still leaves himself as the biggest victim of all.

In time he'd have been on the streets again. The booze-induced activities of Caiozzo and people like him might fit the technical definition of petty crime. But they're the consequence of a public health problem, not just a criminal problem. If anyone could ever stop the menace of public drunkenness as it's committed by such acute addicts, it's more likely to be health professionals than cops or judges or jailers.

This is what society wanted from Caiozzo, and still wants from the dozens of other alcoholics on the streets of Albany. To stop drinking, and to behave. It's not easy, not remotely easy. Not for those whose lives have hit the bottom, and not for the fortunate majority living in their midst, getting hit up for spare change and trying to step over them.

Still, there are simple and reasonable guidelines to follow. It's been 22 years since the state Commission of Correction warned law enforcement and corrections officials alike of the dangers of locking up people who suffer from severe alcoholism. All these years later, it's a warning to take even more seriously.

Of Caiozzo, it might be said that he died at the wrong time, in the wrong place. It might be said as well that it had been years since his life had been on a better track, perhaps not since he was honorably discharged from the service after the Vietnam War, for which he is now honored with his burial in the Saratoga National Veterans Cemetery.

Let his painful and shortened life amount to this much—a lasting reminder of the depths of alcoholism, how to confront that and how not to.

Homeless in Albany

Times Union editorial, November 25, 2002

Homelessness is one of those nagging social problems that doesn't go away. Never has, and never will. What it does, sometimes, is take on a slightly lower profile that makes it harder to notice and easier to ignore. And then, cyclically, it's back in the open, a visible social ill to all but the most callous of eyes.

What alters the balance, then? Around the Capital Region, the colder weather plays a factor, surely. This is when living on the streets, or otherwise underground, goes from a bad existence to a worse one. The holiday season tugs at a more compassionate, and even philosophical, side of many people.

And then there are the homeless themselves. In Albany this month, the passing of one of the more prominent and visible of their ranks was news in its own right. Michael Joseph Earl, dead at 56. Mikey to his family, and "Michael the Archangel" to all who knew him as a steady presence on streets for all those years.

The end of Michael's life, or was it the start of his afterlife, had him in the mainstream, where he hadn't been in a very long time. There he was, waked in a reputable funeral home—good clothes, open casket, and all. There he was, eulogized by a reflective and soft-spoken Methodist minister, the Reverend Maurice Down.

The close to 100 people in attendance included those with weathered faces and worn clothes who may have been closer and more familiar still to Michael and the life he had. And there were those who, at least by appearances, saw and knew Michael at quite a distance.

This one man, down and out and flamboyant all at once, brought those two groups together, at least for an hour or so. But now Michael is gone, as a longtime symbol of what many saw as an endearing side of a nonetheless menacing problem.

It wouldn't have required walking very far from the Central Avenue funeral home that evening to encounter more people who looked like they, too, were homeless, suffering from profound mental health problems, substance abuse, or both. But then it would have been just as easy to retreat to a place where all those haunted lives assigned the single label of homelessness are out of sight.

By the rough, perhaps very rough, estimates of Donna DeMaria of the Homeless Action Committee, the homeless population is up 25 percent from last year, when it was up 24 percent from the previous year. Others, including Public Safety Commissioner John Nielsen, are wary of such estimates.

What's of less dispute is that the shelters are jammed. HAC, in fact, is looking to open another one in January. Places for the likes of Michael the Archangel, people who, as both Ms. DeMaria and Mr. Nielsen note, aren't even known, really, until they're dead.

That means raising money, which HAC—among other groups—does, and attracting volunteers, which it also does.

But it also means raising awareness. "This is an issue that needs to be out there," Ms. DeMaria says.

At least until the next wake. And the one after that.

"No Room for Mercy"

Times Union editorial, September 5, 2003

The inevitable question, the one people will ask but won't answer, came up again in a Rensselaer County courtroom on Wednesday. Why was Christine Wilhelm, so horribly and so indisputably mentally ill, ever on trial for the horrific drowning of one of her young sons and the attempted drowning of the other? Judge Patrick McGrath called further attention to that misapplication of justice as he sentenced Ms. Wilhelm, 39, to the maximum term of 50 years to life in a prison system utterly ill-equipped to treat someone so hopelessly disturbed. The judge's sentence would have come as an afterthought to his acknowledgment of Ms. Wilhelm's condition were it not for its severity. Parole won't even be a faint possibility until she's 86.

"I have no room for mercy in this case," Judge McGrath said. "I agree with the prosecutor that she should be shown the same mercy she showed to Luke and Peter."

What a brutal indictment of the system of laws he is sworn to uphold. The unspeakable crimes against Luke Wilhelm, then 4, and Peter Wilhelm, then 5, cry out for a response that rises above helplessness or revenge.

Just what happens now to Ms. Wilhelm, for whom the system has no mercy? Among the questions that must be asked as she begins a prison sentence that might very well be a death sentence is what treatment for her illness will be available to her, a paranoid schizophrenic? The assertion by District Attorney Patricia DeAngelis that Ms. Wilhelm will receive the help she needs, and should have received long ago, is a puzzling one.

In what way, really, can an institution designed first to punish and only then, perhaps, to rehabilitate possibly accommodate someone who lives in such a frightening fantasy world as Ms. Wilhelm? The confidence of the woman who successfully prosecuted Ms. Wilhelm can't begin to overcome the reservations of mental health experts.

The most immediate concern for Ms. Wilhelm is whether she'll even live very long in prison. She has attempted suicide once already, according to public defender Jerome Frost. It would by no means be inconsistent with the established behavior patterns of mentally ill inmates if she did so again.

Let her sentence begin, then, with the system that showed no mercy for her being properly warned. Christine Wilhelm's protection and well-being are now the state's responsibility. The brutality of her crimes is no excuse for letting her further deteriorate. Nor should it be allowed to stand in the way of an adequate answer for why she was tried and convicted for criminal behavior that she was incapable of controlling.

Editors' note: The Appellate Division of the state Supreme Court overturned Christine Wilhelm's conviction on the basis that Wilhelm's right to counsel was violated during her trial. Among the issues the appellate judges cited in their unanimous ruling: The trial judge, Patrick McGrath, should never have allowed testimony by two child protective case workers who had interviewed Wilhelm without a lawyer. In a plea deal worked out after the appellate ruling, Wilhelm was sent to a secure psychiatric hospital, where she began receiving the treatment for her paranoid schizophrenia that had been impossible for her to obtain in a regular prison. Jerome Frost, the Rensselaer County public defender who represented Wilhelm, died in 2014. He was lauded as a gifted and passionately dedicated attorney who worked tirelessly on behalf of his clients, and the reversal of Christine Wilhelm's conviction was cited as one of his greatest accomplishments in a legal career of 50 years.

Injustice

Times Union Editorial, February 15, 2006

Jon Romano, all of 17, was remarkably composed and articulate when he stood in Rensselaer County Court 14 months ago to be sentenced for attempted murder and reckless endangerment after he fired a shotgun inside Columbia High School.

"I know what I did was wrong, and it was a horrible mistake," he said. "I wish it never happened, but I can't take it back now."

Mr. Romano was absolutely right, about a crime that injured a teacher and left others at his school traumatized. What desperately needs to be taken back, however, is the sentence imposed on him after he entered a guilty plea before Judge Patrick McGrath in November 2004.

Mr. Romano was facing the very real threat of 50 years in prison sought by Patricia DeAngelis, Rensselaer County's merciless district attorney, when he accepted a plea offer of a 20-year sentence against the advice of his lawyer, E. Stewart Jones.

He was, in Mr. Jones's apt description, too young and too frightened to fully realize what he was doing. He also was on medication related to his recent treatment at a psychiatric hospital when he agreed to such a harsh sentence. That, too, may have affected his reasoning.

Mr. Jones should file an appeal on Mr. Romano's behalf, as he says he plans to do. The waiver of the right to an appeal that Ms. DeAngelis insisted Mr. Romano sign should not be an obstacle.

No one disputes that Mr. Romano needs to be punished, in addition to being treated for all that ails him. The issue is the nature and the length of that punishment.

Ms. DeAngelis says the plea bargain that she so adamantly stands by allowed the victims in the case to avoid testifying at a trial and having to go through an ordeal not unlike the day Mr. Romano brought a shotgun to school. There, she has a valid point. But where's her concern for Mr. Romano himself?

Why can't she realize that he was in no position to accept her terms for a plea bargain? Or that Mr. Jones's objections should have been more seriously considered? Or, simply, that she has prevailed in locking up Mr. Romano for too long?

He won't be eligible for parole until he's 33. For that reason, among others, the courts should look upon Mr. Jones's forthcoming appeal with a certain sympathy.

Editors' note: In 2007, the New York State Appellate Division for the Third Judicial District upheld Jon Romano's conviction. He was 17 when he was convicted and

20 when the Appellate Division ruled, and he faced 13 more years in prison before he would become eligible for parole. The district attorney who prosecuted the case, Patricia DeAngelis, did not run for reelection in 2007. She had been the subject of several court admonitions, and her office had been widely criticized for rapid staff turnover, inexperienced assistants, and a reputation for seeking draconian sentences.

A Proud Day for New York

Times Union editorial, June 26, 2011

New Yorkers at last can be proud to know they live in a state that embraces the right of all of its citizens to life, liberty, and the pursuit of happiness. The passage of a same-sex marriage law is about nothing less than that.

It's about allowing two adults who love each other to share their lives—materially and spiritually. New York will no longer deny so many of its citizens the right to enter into this profound and joyous bond, and to enjoy all the benefits that civil marriage brings.

That took leadership.

It took the leadership of those who have fought for this law for years and did not give up.

It took the leadership of the 80 assembly members who approved the bill earlier this month and the 33 senators who finally came through on Friday night to make New York the sixth state, along with the District of Columbia, to declare that a couple's sexual orientation is none of the government's business in deciding who can marry.

It took the leadership of a freshman governor, Andrew Cuomo, and all those who sought the common ground necessary to pass this law.

And it took the tailored narrow compromises that addressed religious concerns while resisting demands to go further at the risk of creating two classes of married people—those protected from discrimination, and those vulnerable to what would have been state-sanctioned bigotry.

With this law, New York rises above a history of homophobia so old and so ingrained that to many people here, and across America, and around the world, it is a virtual truth. It is spoken publicly without shame or apology, passed on from generation to generation. It is shared by people of various faiths and backgrounds, who oppose gay marriage for reasons of religion or tradition or simply a feeling.

It's a bigotry that has been enshrined in the laws or constitutions of 29 states that bar gay marriage, and in the 15-year-old federal Defense of Marriage Act.

And yes, some remnants of this discrimination will be protected in New York for the sake of religion. It's a compromise that a remarkably enduring constitution and reality require. It neither forces those religious groups that condemn gay marriage to honor it, nor bars those that condone it from celebrating it.

Many say this law will harm the institution of marriage. We have yet to hear a convincing argument as to how. If anything, this should strengthen it, allowing more people to marry and giving more citizens a stake in protecting, preserving, and honoring the institution.

While this hardly marks the end of this old prejudice, we can hope that it is another step toward its demise.

The World Owes So Much to Mandela

Times Union opinion piece, December 7, 2013

It requires little more than being of a certain generation, and just a touch of compassion and racial sensitivity, to remain in awe all these years after the magnificent day in 1990 when Nelson Rolihlahla Mandela walked out of an apartheid-era prison and into a new and hopeful day for South Africa and the world watching it.

So went a climatic act in a dizzying three decades of Western history. Civil rights had come, at last and for real, to this country. In Europe, one communist government after another was about to fall. And now this ugly, repressive, institutionalized form of racial cruelty was coming to a forceful but ultimately peaceful end in a land of riches that had been turned into a pariah state.

For that, the world needs to hail Mr. Mandela as it mourns him upon his death at the age of 95. He stands as one of the great crusaders of the 20th century, with the purpose and perseverance of Mahatma Gandhi and the dignity if not necessarily the outward passion and captivating eloquence of Martin Luther King Jr.

"We have waited too long for our freedom," Mr. Mandela said upon his release after more than 27 years in political captivity. "We can wait no longer."

In seemingly no time at all, apartheid was finally over, in a culmination of a struggle that required both guerrilla warfare in the cities and countryside of South Africa and unrelenting diplomatic pressure in the more civilized arena. Apartheid was over, that is, and supplanted by an astonishing triumph of racial rapprochement. Vengeance simply wasn't part of the agenda for the South Africa that Mr. Mandela was about to lead. There, he had the most unlikely of all allies, F. W. de Klerk, the eminently practical Afrikaner who recognized the inevitability of history.

Together they shared the Nobel Peace Prize in 1993.

Here's Mr. Mandela, on that historic occasion:

> We stand here today as nothing more than a representative of the millions of our people who dared to rise up against a social operation whose very essence is war, violence, racism, oppression, repression and the impoverishment of an entire people.

It's useful to remember those words at the end of the life of a man who went from a political dissident so feared that incarceration was deemed necessary to a statesman revered at home and abroad.

It's for good reason that the prison cell where Mr. Mandela so ironically grew in power and influence is destined to be a sacred place for the ages. That's where, as President Barack Obama wrote by way of introduction to Mr. Mandela's 2010 book of letters, "even when little sunlight shined into that Robben Island cell, he could see a better future—one worthy of sacrifice."

There's not a country anywhere where such vision and perseverance won't help bring about better days.

Editors' note: Jim wrote this opinion piece when Nelson Mandela was hospitalized in grave condition earlier in 2013. The *Times Union* held the piece when Mandela recovered. When Mandela did die, on December 5, 2013, the *Times Union* ran Jim's tribute to him, with this note to readers at the end of the piece: *Jim McGrath was chief editorial writer for the Times Union until his death September 4. He wrote this as an editorial when Nelson Mandela was hospitalized in grave condition earlier this year.*

(Page 99)

Jim in one of his most familiar poses: studying the headlines and Page 1 design of the day's newspaper offerings in the news boxes on a street corner in Chicago's Lakeview neighborhood, near Wrigley Field, in this photograph from October 2004. Chicago was Jim's second-favorite city, and he knew it very well. He graduated from Lake Forest College, in Lake Forest, Illinois, a half hour north of Chicago, and earned his master's degree at Northwestern University's Medill School of Journalism, in Evanston, on Chicago's northern boundary. He returned to Chicago many times later in his life, and his courtship with Darryl began there, after Darryl left the *Times Union* in 1998 and moved to Chicago for a yearlong midcareer internship with the *Chicago Tribune*. Photograph by Darryl McGrath.

JOURNALISM

Introduction

McGrath Thought That Newspapers Ought to Tell the Truth

Dan Lynch

Jim McGrath had funny ideas about newspapers—or, at least, funny ideas in this shoddy era of lying social media posts and flagrant untruths about public affairs in all sorts of forums. McGrath thought that newspapers ought to tell the truth.

Or, more precisely, he thought that a newspaper should offer readers the best available version of facts presented in fair, full, and proper context and to express its opinions on those facts fearlessly and ferociously. McGrath felt that a newspaper was no place for fiction. He was disturbed by lazy writing and by the expression of careless, fuzzy thought. He was annoyed by the display of weak or half-baked opinions, especially on the editorial page.

The McGrath pieces that follow this introduction illustrate vividly his thinking along those lines and the rigor of the standards that he brought both to his own written work and to the study of the work of others. As was virtually always true of his work, these articles were crafted with the clarity of thought and the forceful phrasing with which McGrath virtually always presented his points. His arguments were carefully considered and displayed an enviable depth of perception concerning his subject. As for his phrasing and mastery of language, many professional writers familiar with his work, myself included, often found ourselves reading McGrath and muttering privately to ourselves, "I wish that I'd written that."

McGrath always stood tall against the inevitable degradation of journalistic standards that accompanied the decline of printed newspapers in the Internet age. The son of a newspaper printer, he often railed in private against the growing perception of the printed newspaper merely as an inky relic of the industrial age. He understood that as a newspaper staff declined, so, too, would the quality of the product that staff produced. That was why he wrote so often about the need for newspapers to be better than they had ever been, to adhere to rigorous standards, to struggle harder day by day to maintain quality.

The pieces that follow this introduction include an evaluation of a Maine newspaper that McGrath produced that could well serve as a brief journalism text. His observations and assessments of that newspaper's strengths and weaknesses were both sharp and directly on point. Equally powerful is his assessment of *Boston Globe* columnists Mike Barnicle and Patricia Smith and the shortcomings that led each to new careers outside the *Globe*. His evaluation of the career of Pulitzer Prize–winning writer J. Anthony Lukas shows similar perception, as well as empathy for a man who simply tried too hard. That depth of perception carries over to the piece he produced on the work of the late Mike Royko, the leading newspaper voice of Chicago for decades.

What shows through clearly in all these pieces is the deep affection and respect that McGrath felt for both his own work and the work of others in print journalism. What also shows through is his continual dissatisfaction with the shortcomings of his profession and his desire to do whatever he could to make it better, stronger, and of ever-better service to its readers. In the end, that's who McGrath cared about—the readers of the newspaper and the effect that newspapers had upon the democratic process that's the basis of our lives as Americans.

Dan Lynch was a journalist and author. He spent a decade as host of his own daily, three-hour, drive-time talk radio program on two Albany radio stations. He hosted his own Sunday morning public affairs program on Albany's NBC television affiliate. He served as both managing editor and featured columnist for the Albany *Times Union*. He was chief political writer for the *Philadelphia Inquirer* and New York editor of *Newsday*. His documentary film work has been seen on the History Channel and on local TV. He was a graduate of the Temple University School of Journalism and the author of 13 books. He died of cancer June 4, 2017.

Royko was the Real People's Court

Times Union opinion piece, May 1, 1997

Two decades or so ago, a Chicago newspaperman named Mike Royko was doing the best thing you can do in this business: putting the powerful and the arrogant in their place and then writing about it for the rest of us.

His 1971 book, *Boss*, about the political thuggery of Mayor Richard J. Daley, so powerful that he may well have surpassed even Erastus Corning and Dan O'Connell on that score, still stands out as one of the great books about big-city American politics.

Jimmy Breslin hailed it as a book that "comes at you from the saloons and neighborhoods, the police stations and political backrooms. It is about lies and viciousness, about the worship of cement and the hatred toward blacks, about troubling cowardice that hides behind religion and patriotism while the poor get clubbed and killed."

Chicago *Reader* press critic Michael Miner described Royko the other day as the court of appeals for the people who wouldn't otherwise get a fair hearing in a city so parochial and corrupt.

To think Royko wasn't even 40 when he wrote *Boss*. He never did another book, either, just collections of his newspaper columns.

With his death now at 64, the toasts and tributes come in for the man whose newspaper column invented the likes of Slats Grobnick and Dr. I. M. Kookie. But the truth, sad to say, is that Royko had lost a step or three. His health was falling apart. There was a very public and very messy DWI. He had long since moved out of the neighborhood, and the city, too, for one of the Waspy suburbs to the north.

At times his column had a mean streak, particularly toward gays and Hispanics. Royko became the subject of some harsh criticism, around town, by Miner in the *Reader*, and once even in the *Wall Street Journal*. Oh, he'd connect enough, so that his column ran, it seemed, in papers everywhere, and often on this very page.

In his day, Royko's column was something people instinctively grabbed on to, like a subway car strap. It hung above the only city he ever lived in, like the Chicago poet Carl Sandburg's fog or his writer friend Nelson Algren's broad shoulders.

He was good enough to have won a Pulitzer at his first paper, the long-dead *Chicago Daily News*, and made a good bit of news when he left his second one, the *Chicago Sun-Times*, for the *Chicago Tribune* because he wouldn't work for one Rupert Murdoch, known in Royko's columns as "The Alien."

Hard as it is to pick his best moment, try this one. It was, again, two decades ago, Daley's machine-picked successor, a party hack named Michael Bilandic, was ousted in the 1979 Democratic primary for reason enough to bring down any mayor. The town that prided itself as "The City That Works" just hadn't delivered during a winter of relentless snow.

Royko wrote his column the day after that election for the folks who stood in the cold waiting for subway trains that never came and for those whose streets were never plowed. "You, you, you, you, and you . . . ," Royko wrote, in the hour of the triumph and the revenge of the most ordinary people.

That was him, all right. If Royko is to be remembered now, far from home, best it be for work like that.

J. Anthony Lukas

Times Union editorial, June 10, 1997

It's hard to imagine a sadder story. The writer J. Anthony Lukas is dead, at just 64, and by his own doing. He took his life not long after finishing his latest book, which he didn't think was very good.

His agent, Amanda Urban, insists that the book, about a turn-of-the-century murder trial in the West, was outstanding. We'll take her at her word.

The fact is that Mr. Lukas was an extraordinary writer, one of the best of his generation at nonfiction. He won a Pulitzer Prize for his 1985 book *Common Ground*, which was all about what happened when the public schools in Boston were desegregated under federal court order a decade earlier. Anyone who knows anything at all about Boston will assure you that those were ugly, terrible times that nearly ruined a city and made its bad schools even worse.

Mr. Lukas was a notorious perfectionist. It took him seven years to write that book, which gets deep into Boston's core, revealing almost everything there is to know about its people, its neighborhoods, its politics, its dominant newspaper and its almighty church. For that work alone he deserves to be remembered as a man of enormous insight and boundless energy.

Oh, there were other well-received books—one about the kids of the 1960s, one about the Chicago Seven trial, and an excellent one about Nixon and Watergate—and a stretch as well at the *New York Times*, where his reporting won an earlier Pulitzer. He was president of the Authors Guild and was one of the big-name participants in a 1991 conference on nonfiction writing at the University at Albany that people who care about that sort of thing are still talking about. An impressive life all around, haunted as it was.

Finding Fame in Telling Fibs

Times Union opinion piece, July 10, 1998

This one is all about lying. The sad truth is that it's evolving into a lucrative and worthwhile practice, particularly so in our own business. Seventeen years ago, one made-up newspaper story was all it took to transform Janet Cooke from one of journalism's rising stars into the absolute nobody that she remains even today. Harsh? Hardly. Such was the price she had to pay for telling the readers of the *Washington Post* the singular but outrageous lie of the life of a nonexistent 8-year-old heroin addict.

Now here comes Patricia Smith—celebrity liar, multiple offender, and, maddeningly, emerging literary star.

Smith is giving a reading Saturday night in Washington Park in Albany. Her poetry and fiction act lives on, even after she was dumped from her job as a columnist for the *Boston Globe*. At least four of her columns, published over a course of less than two months, were fiction—but presented as fact. All about people who never existed and events that never happened.

Another 48 of her columns are officially suspect, according to the *Globe*. It's far and away the worst sin imaginable in journalism.

Not that Smith is bothered by her newfound infamy. In a farewell column that the *Globe* inexplicably printed, she struck a defiant tone. "I will survive this knowing that the heart of my columns was honest and heartfelt. . . . I will write as long as I breathe, despite the dire predictions that this indiscretion spells the end of my career."

But first Smith wants to cash in on the very disgrace that she has brought about, on her newspaper and on herself. She tells one of our own reporters that she's looking to write and market a novel. The timing is just right, she says.

Smith wouldn't be the first literary liar to treat falsehoods like winning lottery tickets. Remember Joe Klein? He was the pouting baby boomer of a magazine writer who made a splashy novel out of his worship-turned-disenchantment toward Bill Clinton. What a smashing literary gimmick that one was. For months, the book was a best-seller, while Klein repeated, again and again, the self-serving lie that he was not the author named "Anonymous." Not long after the truth came out, thanks to some good old-fashioned journalism in the *Washington Post*, Klein got a job as a writer for the *New Yorker*, a magazine that used to have very different standards.

To think that, now, Smith may outdo Klein. If she plays it right and packages it right, getting fired for making up newspaper stories could turn out to be the best thing that ever happened to a career that knows no shame. Like she'll really miss work that she already dismisses by comparing a life in journalism to a life selling insurance.

And Saturday night she plays Albany. Oh, she has every right to do a reading here. That's one of the other sacred rules by which this business is supposed to live. It's just that anyone who cares about the integrity and credibility that ought to accompany good writing—anyone, in fact, who prefers not to be a pawn of someone else's self-promotion—should stay away.

Mike Barnicle's Sad Fall from Grace to Disgrace

Times Union opinion piece, August 8, 1998

Eileen McNamara, a *Boston Globe* columnist with her reputation deservedly intact, wrote recently that she started at the paper as a secretary around the same time Mike Barnicle began as a columnist. It's true. For Barnicle, starting at the bottom meant taking one of the great jobs in the business. That was 25 years ago, when he was just turning 30, a few years off the speech-writing staff of Robert Kennedy.

For all that time, Barnicle could be a very good columnist—when he wanted to be, and when he worked at it. Some of the early columns still resonate. When Boston was struggling, and badly so, with an ill-conceived plan to desegregate its public schools, Barnicle took on a right-wing talk radio host named Avi Nelson, who was trying to rally and exploit the racist elements in the anti-busing movement.

The good columns showed sound instincts and perseverance. Barnicle spent time in neighborhoods that otherwise tended to be overlooked by a paper that has a stunning ability to not quite connect with its own city and what should be the core of its readership. He made the point, again and again, that without a decent public school system, there was no such thing as a middle class and thus not much of a city. He reiterated that sound social policy without full employment was an oxymoron. He had a good handle on the big political players in Boston—the Kennedys, the late Paul Tsongas, and, for a time, an ambitious governor named Michael Dukakis.

His columns could alternately be very funny and quite moving. We occasionally ran them on this page.

But Barnicle's columns also could be disappointing, infuriatingly so. That was the case, especially, in more recent years. There were lame columns about getting older and the lousy sex life that came with it. There were his entirely juvenile columns about Viagra. There were columns that just didn't say anything.

Barnicle also had a parochial streak. He took digs at Albany without any evidence that he's ever been anywhere near here, and in stark ignorance of the reality that a Boston guy with such a keen interest in politics is going to find this to be a rather fascinating place.

He seemed, and not at all unlike some other columnists, far more interested in being on TV and occasionally radio, too, entertaining audiences with insights that are as glib as they might be articulate.

For the August 2 edition of the Sunday paper, Barnicle submitted an utterly uninspired list of one-liners. Worse, the *Globe* published it.

Turns out that eight of the gag lines were all but identical to some in a bestselling book by the comedian George Carlin. For this Barnicle gives a tortured explanation. He hadn't read Carlin's book, he said, though he had plugged it on TV. He got his material from a bartender, he said. That qualified as reporting, apparently.

Barnicle said he was always on the hunt for one-liners. "I collect them on cocktail napkins, in notebooks, by e-mail till I have nothing to write on a nice, hot summer weekend," he told the *Washington Post*.

The disciplinary part of all this—the paper wants his resignation and he's told them where to go—is the smaller part of this sad story. The inconsistencies in Barnicle's account of how Carlin became his coauthor are enough to make him guilty of dishonesty.

The bigger problem is what's become of the larger body of his work. The *Globe* has a writer on its hands who no longer is writing very well, and certainly not with any consistency.

Meanwhile, Barnicle has taken refuge in the role of martyr. He's presenting himself, at the low point of his career, as the victim of a business that has much more serious flaws. Barnicle says his sins are nothing compared to those of Patricia Smith, who was fired from her job as a *Globe* columnist in June after it became apparent that she routinely was writing columns that were complete fiction. He's right, of course, on that count. But how pathetic it is that the best Barnicle can say for himself is that Smith is a worse case than he is.

From grace to disgrace. Barnicle has handed his bosses another dose of the most uncomfortable sort of attention a paper can attract. Already there's grumbling that by trying to get rid of Barnicle, the *Globe* is engaging in what amounts to affirmative action for troublesome columnists. The truth is there's something to that. After a black woman gets fired for being a liar, Barnicle, as a white Irish male, invites harsher punishment than he otherwise might have received. It's hard to imagine the *Globe* wanting Barnicle out of the paper permanently if Smith hadn't been banished from there as well.

So add bad timing to Barnicle's rap sheet. He already was under intense scrutiny, by his editors and readers alike. Just when he should have been more diligent, he instead was more careless.

In his future travels—to the lawyers' offices to fight it out with the *Globe*, or to journalism's equivalent of the glue factory—Barnicle might think of how he had it all, and how he tossed it all away.

There's no need now to visit Albany, either. When was the last time his column ran here? For that matter, when might be the next time?

Editorial and Op-Ed Page Critique of the
Portland Press Herald and *Maine Sunday Telegram*

August 1999

Editors' note: Jim McGrath wrote the following critique of two Maine newspapers to accompany his application for an editorial position with them. The only known copy of the critique was found in Jim's desk in the *Times Union* newsroom after his death. A few words are missing from the original text, the result of the columns running over the margins on a page. We decided to include the critique because it speaks so well to Jim's philosophy of editorial writing. We have marked the sections where text is missing and reconstructed a few sentence fragments as best we could. Jim did not get the job (hardly surprising when you read his unsparingly honest critique), but his straightforward assessment stands as a tribute to his high standards and passion for clear, forceful, and effective editorial writing.

It's best to begin with this caveat. I'm well aware of how much easier it is for me to spread a week's worth of papers across my kitchen table, read them over, and write a critique that isn't entirely complimentary.

Twenty years in the newspaper business have taught me many indelible lessons, among them how hard it is to do good work under such demanding circumstances, day after day after day. I also acknowledge that I'd be inclined to be a bit wary of criticism offered by someone from a paper not much bigger and possibly no better.

That said, here goes.

The editorial page of the *Portland Press Herald* and the *Maine Sunday Telegram* is perfectly OK. The writing is clear and serious in tone, if not especially bold. The observations are sharp, even if the positions the page takes are restrained, sometimes puzzlingly so. Irreverence is missing and so, too, is any trace of a sense of humor.

At its best, the editorial page conveys a strong sense of place. The expertise on environmental matters is particularly impressive. The George's Bank editorial (Sunday, August 8) is one example. The one on the National Resources Council of Maine and the battle for the Allagash (Monday, August 9) is another. M. D. Harmon's column (Sunday, August 8) on the global warming scare is yet another. Other times, though, parochialism is more apparent, as in the editorial on Acadia National Park (Sunday, August 8).

If there's a consistent weakness in the editorials, it's a failure to make your arguments stronger and present them more thoroughly. Maybe that means longer editorials on occasion. I like tight writing and count myself among the great admirers of Richard Aregood. But slightly longer editorials can be to the point as well. It's admirable that a small staff can write three editorials a day, every day. But just two editorials that are even better might be preferable sometimes.

The lobster fishing piece (Monday, August 9) and the land use editorial (Sunday, August 8) are examples of what would be very good editorials if only they said more. Just how lax is Maine's regulation of the lobster industry? How egregious are the violations? Is there a state that does have effective laws?

I certainly have no sympathy for the two guys who were arrested and named in the [missing text]. I want to know more and read more. A certain amount of background is given to readers, of course, but surely this is an enormously important issue in Maine. I suspect that lobstermen are a powerful, or at least a very loud and visible, interest group. Show them. Get rid of the file photo that adds nothing to the page visually if indeed art is warranted. Lay out just what would be acceptable lobster fishing laws and keep [missing text].

Your case for more suitable laws restricting property subdivisions is similarly muted, I'm afraid. This problem might not be as well publicized as the eroding lobster resources. An example or two of development hell would bolster this editorial considerably. And what is the answer? Vermont, for instance, has a very strong statewide land use law. It's not very popular in the predictable quarters, but I'd argue that Vermont is a much-better-off place because of Act 250 (as I believe it's called.) Is that the way to go in Maine? Or is it realistic to think that smaller towns would be able to adequately enforce tougher planning and zoning laws?

Again, I assume that yet more special interests—namely, developers, contractors, and perhaps even the building trade unions—stand in opposition to the paper's position. Your editorial stance, then, needs to be especially firm. (An aside: You mention a state housing shortage. In Maine? An ideal editorial page topic to be examined at length, I'd think.) The proposed Cumberland County sports arena is still another instance where I'd expect the paper to be bolder and more assertive in its views. Personally, I have reservations about government by referendum and initiative. (It's been a disaster, it seems clear, in California and Massachusetts.) But if you are convinced that voter approval should be required before an arena is built, then say so, say why, and say it more forcefully.

Your editorial (Thursday, August 12) is a weak one. You back into it, complete with the almost cliché of a scolding about missed opportunities. You're way too deferential to those who you think are conducting bad public policy. (Example: "They should ask anyway.") It's good, I suppose, to know that Councilors Geraghty and Cloutier also want to hold a vote on the funding of the arena. But why aren't you more critical of a mayor who'd spend $46 million in public money without one?

And just where does the paper stand on building the arena at all? An earlier editorial (Friday, August 6) makes much of all the work that the Capitalization Committee has to do. Even if this private outfit comes up with $20 million or even $30 million, that's still a lot of money at stake, as the later editorial makes clear.

I certainly hope that by the time these meetings began on August 17 you had offered your readers at least a hint of your leanings. Otherwise, the paper's voice in such an important and ongoing debate will be all but irrelevant.

Other editorials fail to make even wishy-washy arguments. What are you trying to say, for example, about William Cohen's warning about terrorism (Monday, August 9) other than to repeat what he already said in a column in your own paper? The editorial on federal and city debt (Saturday, August 7), awkward transition and all, has me further confused about what you're trying to say about what's admittedly a very complicated topic.

At least one position you took was quite naive, I thought. Of course parents need to save for their kids' college educations (Saturday, August 7). My fear is that the tuition savings plan Maine is considering will encourage higher college costs more than anything else. The Harvards and the Yales, and the Bowdoins and the Colbys, are likely to see more money set aside well in advance of kids' enrollment and raise their prices accordingly. The *Chronicle of Higher Education*, for one, has expressed such skepticism about college savings plans. At the very least, I think your editorial needed to offer examples of how such plans made college more affordable. Decades of tuition increases well in excess of the rate of inflation are cause for wariness toward any purported solution.

None of the criticisms are meant to suggest that most of your editorials are flawed. Some, like the one on the Standish town councilor, are precisely what editorials should be—clear, convincing, and fair. Strong editorials about such local topics (what other daily paper is going to comment on Betty Dolloff, I wonder) are what ultimately will distinguish your page.

Many papers, my own included, commented on the pediatricians' group's call to wean very young kids off TV. Your editorial was perhaps the best one I read of all.

The op-ed page is more varied, even more adventurous, than the editorial page but also more inconsistent. Without question, the local perspective is the page's strength. M. D. Harmon's and John Porter's columns, to judge by just one of each, display knowledge and authority.

Does Peter Black write regularly? I hope so. He offers an interesting perspective. Meikie Jenness might have something equally intriguing to say. Her column (Thursday, August 12) rambled, though. I'm far more curious about her comparisons of Maine and Swaziland than I am about her rather unfocused media criticism. Nancy Grape laments the obvious (Sunday, August 8) that lobbyists have bought one congressman after another. A stronger piece would suggest how to bring this collective industry of special interests under control. As for the syndicated writers, I applaud you for running Paul Greenberg. He's a relentless critic of everything Clinton, of course, but he's also a very credible one. The country should have at least listened to him, oh, seven or eight years ago. Clarence Page isn't a bad choice for (I assume) a regular writer, too. Too bad his column (Friday, August 6) reacting to Hillary Clinton's *Talk* magazine interview wasn't remotely reflective of his better work.

Otherwise, though, the page seems to be like so many op-ed pages. Full of the usual suspects. In your case, that's David Broder, George Will, and Ellen Goodman. Perhaps I've been reading all three of them for too long. They just don't interest me much anymore. Kathleen Parker never interested me, and I can see and hear Cynthia Tucker often enough on the Jim Lehrer program.

As a subscriber to the New York Times News Service, you have several good columnists available for free, namely, Frank Rich, William Safire, and, now, Gail Collins. I applaud you, though, for passing on Maureen Dowd.

Getting the ads off the op-ed page is out of the question, I fear. Their presence is far from your only problem with—what's the hot term now?—design, presentation, etc., however. The pages are too busy. A label/overline, a traditional headline and then a subhead/readout is way too much. On your shortest editorial, the heads and the rest seem to say almost as much as the text itself. Readouts in letters to the editor pose a similar but more serious problem. The excessive use of photos, especially on the editorial page, rarely adds anything. Certainly, there's a place, even a need, for art on these pages. Words, though, should come first. Even then, art shouldn't look like a space-filling device. The masthead, finally, is so big as to be unwieldy. The various info boxes you use are useful, of course, but they also could stand to be smaller and more concise.

Fortunately, the design problems would be quite easy to solve. The weaknesses with the writing might be more challenging. With a staff committed to a better editorial and op-ed page, however, yours could easily be an industry [ending missing].

Reality Check at Skidmore

Times Union editorial, November 16, 1999

Perhaps the most enlightening lesson of the semester at Skidmore College comes outside the classroom. It's one for the students, who along with their parents pay big money to go there, but especially for the adults, who get paid to know better.

It's that you can't crush the truth and you can't alter reality. So you shouldn't try.

What happened on the Saratoga Springs campus was unsettling. To pretend that it didn't occur was to deny reality.

A student's truck, bearing a gay-identified sticker, was vandalized outside a dorm for gay students. Smeared with human feces, to be graphically blunt about it.

The student paper, the *Skidmore News*, was properly disgusted by such an act. On that, the students and the administration, which began investigating a potential hate crime, were of like minds.

The *Skidmore News* report of the incident includes stark photos and language ("The ____ That Happens: Reacting to Hate," a headline read), and thoughtful commentary.

It was too much for the director of admissions, Mary Lou Bates. She had the paper—actually about 1,200 copies, just over half the usual press run—taken off campus, lest it shock or otherwise offend prospective students and their parents at an open house last Monday.

Ms. Bates has since apologized and rather profusely so.

Skidmore is a small school, where word travels fast. Hiding the paper wasn't going to keep anyone from knowing what was happening on campus. Nor was what occurred likely to keep anyone from wanting to attend Skidmore. A prospective student who couldn't handle this situation most likely wouldn't belong there in the first place.

There are gays and there are those who are uptight about gays on every college campus. Skidmore seemed to be dealing with this unpleasant incident just fine—until the papers vanished.

The public perception problem that motivated Ms. Bates is worse now, of course. But it's nothing Skidmore can't get over, as long as it confronts matters rather than pretend they don't exist.

Class dismissed.

SPORTS

(Page 115)

Although Jim's family favored ice hockey, Jim became a soccer player. He learned the game from the sons of European and South American immigrants in his Brighton neighborhood in Boston. He went on to play for the Division III Lake Forest College team and helped it win two Midwestern Conference championships. Here, in this undated photograph, Jim wears the uniform of Boston Latin School, the highly selective, specialized, public high school in Boston that required an entrance exam, and from which Jim graduated. Photograph courtesy of E. F. X. Cusack.

Introduction

A Red Sox Fan Above All

Phillip Blanchard

I met Jim McGrath in 1988, when he was working for the Albany *Knickerbocker News* and I was at the *Times Union*. The *Knick*, an afternoon newspaper, was in its dying days. I was a copy editor for the *TU*. As our crew headed out for the night, he would appear at the desk (the two papers shared work space), apparently to pick and edit wire stories for the *Knick*, which was printed in the early morning. I never really knew what he was doing.

He kept to himself during these encounters. For all I know, he was checking sports scores.

McGrath (I always called him by his last name, and he called me by mine), when the *Knick* folded, moved to the *TU* desk. I quickly learned what a good editor he was.

But it wasn't until April 13, 1989, that I learned what a sports fan he was.

I joined a carload of other *Times Union* editors that day for a trip to Fenway Park. McGrath was the leader. Somehow, he was able to walk up to a ticket window and get us seats behind home plate. It was an afternoon game, Red Sox versus Cleveland. Roger Clemens was on the mound for the Sox. Clemens got his first win of the year, outpitching the hapless Rich Yett and leading his team to a 9-1 victory.

It was the first time I saw Major League Baseball in person. What an introduction, seeing the Rocket in action and having McGrath's running commentary on the game and the crowd. He was energized in his element. I knew that if I was going to see baseball, he would be my best companion. And he was.

After I left the *TU* later that year for Chicago, McGrath became a *Times Union* editorial writer. He branched into occasional column writing; his focus was on politics, yet it was clear that he had the most fun writing about sports.

Reporting from "the western fringe of Sox Nation," much of his baseball writing was naturally focused on his beloved team. But knowing that his audience was mostly in Yankees and Mets territory, he tipped his hat to local loyalties, even acknowledging that Joe Torre, the Yankees' manager, was "the statesman of baseball."

McGrath was a Red Sox fan above all, but he reveled in visiting ballparks other than Fenway. But even as he wrote about one of his out-of-town trips, he acknowledged that baseball was not indispensable. He might have been joking.

The piece "A Spectator's View from the Seats" is Roger Angell–caliber writing.

McGrath wrote about other sports, too, but more dispassionately. It is telling that the two football-related editorials here were focused on a marching band and pedophilia. There was no kindness there.

The year before the old Comiskey Park in Chicago was torn down, McGrath and I went to a game there. The White Sox pitcher managed to walk in four runs in the first inning. As a fan, I was appalled. As a bystander in Chicago, McGrath just said something like, "Isn't that the damnedest thing." I wish he had written about the game. He would have had a lot more to say.

Phillip Blanchard was a reporter at the Albany *Times Union* from 1972 to 1974, and a copy editor from 1986 to 1989. He later was a copy editor at the *Chicago Sun-Times* from 1989 to 2000, and then at the *Washington Post* from 2000 to 2008. He is now an independent editor. He lives in Albuquerque, New Mexico.

Introduction

"Hey, Jim, How Does Yaz Spell His Name?"

Howard Healy

When it came to sports, Jim and I were the archetypal Odd Couple. Jim was the Oscar Madison type, scores, stats, and lore at his fingertips. ("Hey Jim, how does Yaz spell his name?" Jim, without turning his head or missing a stroke on his keyboard, would call out the letters. It was like having my personal sports Google.)

I was the neophyte, my sole interest in sports being the Washington Redskins, an addiction I acquired when working in Washington during the era of Coach George Allen, who had managed to shape the previously hapless team into a Super Bowl contender. While I knew so little about sports, Jim seemed to know everything. The pieces that follow will attest to that. I also learned a lot from him through our casual conversations, which I am sharing here for the first time.

As far as I could tell, Jim did not have a favorite NFL team, although he had vast knowledge of the game and the league. He also had a broad view of pro football as a microcosm of real life, particularly when it involved issues of discrimination. When Doug Williams became the first black quarterback to win a Super Bowl, Jim was as much of a Redskins fan as I was. And when Doug Flutie, the Boston College star, made his triumphant return to the NFL after a long detour in the CFL, Jim was there to cheer on the quarterback that so many NFL coaches had spurned as being too small to be "our guy."

Football aside, Jim's real sports love—as anyone who knew him even casually was aware—was baseball. That's baseball as spelled Boston Red Sox, and it was a consuming love. Jim was a loyal member of Red Sox nation, and his knowledge of the team and its lore was, to a neophyte like me, mesmerizing. I remember one instance in particular when Jim's influence on me was on display. It happened on a day when Jim had called in sick and I was assigned to write an editorial about a Red Sox–Yankees game that was pivotal in the race for the pennant. I don't recall much of what I wrote except that I slipped in a line to the effect that the Red Sox were the more authentic team of the two (meaning that the Bronx boys always had the cash to buy the best talent, and "buy" championships, while the Red Sox would have to earn victory on their own merits). You can imagine the reaction from Yankee fans, who lit up the switchboard the following morning. It wasn't pretty, but it was worth it to see that sly grin on Jim's face when he returned to work that day.

Jim had an interest in many other sports, of course, and it would take too long to mention them all in this limited space. Here's a partial list:

Soccer. Jim played soccer in high school and college and, in one Walter Mitty moment, confided in me that he thought his kicking leg was strong enough to win him a spot as a kicker in the NFL. Besides being a good soccer player, Jim was also an observer of how soccer could reflect the worst in society. In one telling example, Jim recalled his Boston days when his team played a team in a minority neighborhood and the players needed a police escort to return home amid the bigots who were waiting to hurl invective. Soccer also exposed—perhaps more than any other sport—the huge gap between media coverage and pay for women athletes compared with men. Jim hated those double standards.

Basketball, or "Hoops" in Jim's language. I never saw anyone who could fill out a March Madness grid as quickly and authoritatively as Jim. Though we rarely talked basketball in the office—except when Siena was in the March Madness mix—when Jim did discuss the game, he sometimes sounded like a character straight out of *Hoosiers*.

Boxing. When Mike Tyson was a presence in the Capital Region and on his way to becoming heavyweight champ, he developed a signature mantra—"I just wanna box"—which he delivered in a high-pitched staccato. Jim could mimic that mantra with perfect pitch and cadence.

Horse racing. The last time I saw Jim alive was shortly before Travers day, when we had lunch on a Saturday at a local diner. As we were leaving, Jim gave me a slip of paper with an exacta bet for the Travers—names and numbers that meant nothing to me. Even so, I placed the bet and then forgot about it, assuming I would never see that $5 again. I was wrong. The morning after the Travers I opened my newspaper to find that Jim's horses had come in, just as he said they would. I remember picking up my princely winnings of $60 and asking myself how I ever could have doubted Jim. After all, when he gave you a tip on a sport—any sport—it was a good one. Bet on that.

A Spectator's View from the Seats

Times Union, Sports, July 23, 1995

The baseball season has moved into its second half and stumbled, if you believe the gloom-and-doom crowd and the notion that the game is finished, which has taken on a relentlessness of its own. It's not unlike the speculation over Cal Ripken's streak of consecutive games. Cal breaks Gehrig's record, then the whole game dies. Oh, the critics have discovered their obligatory new star in Hideo Nomo, but otherwise the story of baseball has become a story of dreary attendance figures and low TV ratings.

Attendance is down; everyone knows that by now, especially in the small-market towns that the strike was largely about in the first place. At other parks in other cities it's not that bad, actually. The fans are still coming and the games still tend to be exciting. There are enclaves of hope out there.

A lot of it is perspective. Forget the press boxes and the luxury boxes. What's it like in the stands, where the fans pay for their own tickets and buy their own refreshments?

I went on the road for six games in three parks in nine days. This is what I saw.

FENWAY PARK, BOSTON, JUNE 18

Wouldn't you know that the Red Sox would be the one team whose attendance would actually be up in the season after the strike. Fenway Park itself is at once a temple of hope and despair, where generations of Red Sox fans have waited in vain for the team to win it all. This year, the Sox are off to a surprisingly good start. So, the fans keep coming back into what's both the smallest and oldest park in the big leagues, full of legacy and charm but a bit short on comfort.

On this Sunday, the team is actually in its first real slump of the season, three losses in a row, and eight losses in 10 games, which is duly noted in both Boston papers. The question lingers: Just how serious is this? The Sox have one more chance to beat the Milwaukee Brewers before their homestand ends, and an announced attendance of 28,648, a few thousand less, most likely, than would be there when the pennant race really picks up, is on hand on a sweltering day. The Sox take an early lead and then lose it. There seems to be restlessness mixed with the rather intense interest in the game that you'll almost always find here.

Fenway becomes alive, finally, in the seventh inning, on a Tim Naehring homer, a sacrifice fly and a bad play in the Brewers' outfield. It's enough for a 4-2 Sox lead. The bullpen, a source of anguish for Sox fans this year and many years, holds the lead, and the level of cynicism seems surprisingly low. A guy deep in the back of

Section 10, along the right-field line between first base and the foul pole, is sarcastic in his speculation, but it's really nothing compared to the way Sox fans can second-guess the manager to death and even explore ways that the game could be lost.

But it's a win, and the fans are content as they head out into Kenmore Square, to the subway, the highways, and beyond. A few hours later, the area around the ballpark has emptied out, and on a walk down Landsdown Street, behind the Green Monster, the talk accepts the inevitable that a new Fenway Park isn't much more than a few years away and speculates as to just what will happen to old Fenway.

Comisky Park, Chicago, June 21–25

OK, baseball can be boring at times. A Thursday afternoon game between the White Sox and the Seattle Mariners drives that point home. The Mariners are without Ken Griffey, who's injured, and their other great draw, Randy Johnson, pitched two nights earlier. The White Sox have been, to this point, a huge disappointment, leading the league in errors and perhaps nothing else. A complete game by Sox pitcher Jim Abbott is wasted. When it comes time to show the White Sox's best play of the game on the huge TV screen in center field, it's of John Kruk, now a cancer survivor and chubby and scruffy as ever, belting one into the left field corner and easing up as he takes second base for a double.

The White Sox lose, 3-2. Attendance is low, 20,836, a bit less than the major league average. The next night, the Cleveland Indians, the hottest team in baseball, come into town for the first of three games. This is the sort of rivalry that should absolutely thrive under baseball's new three-division format, the sort of series White Sox fans should have been marking on their calendars sometime around the start of spring training. But a 17½-game gap between these teams in the Central Division standings has a way of taking some luster off the upcoming weekend at Comiskey. The big thing on the Chicago sports pages is the upcoming NBA draft.

But guess what? More than 90,000 people, including a season high on Saturday night, see the Sox sweep the series. That averages out to better than the White Sox drew for all of last season. For two hot nights, and then on a steamy Sunday, the crowds are engaged, animated, and well behaved.

On Friday night, the Sox erupt for 20 hits. Frank Thomas, the fans' favorite, hits his 16th homer and has three RBI, and Kruk has three more hits and three RBI in an 12-5 win. Attendance is 31,962, a season's best for all of a day.

People can talk all they want about how quaint it is at Wrigley Field, up on the North Side of town where the Cubs play, but Comiskey takes it hands down when it comes to comfort and accessibility. Easy to get to, by car or, better yet, subway. Easy to walk around in. Big seats, wide aisles, and plenty of concession stands. The stadium is just four years old, a notch below the architectural rages of Camden Yards in Baltimore and Jacobs Field in Cleveland, but generations ahead of those big symmetrical bowls in places such as Philadelphia and Cincinnati. We watch Saturday's game from the upper deck above third base. An interesting vantage point, and suggestive that there really isn't a bad seat in the park. In front of us are six Indians fans who speak little English, aside from wondering who's responsible for driving home. They smile constantly and for nine innings never meet a vendor they don't like. You name it. Beer, pizza, hot dogs, peanuts.

Alex Fernandez goes the distance for the Sox, and strikes out 11 in an 8-3 win. For once it's the other team making the errors. The Indians make four of them, including two by left fielder Albert Belle, who actually looks a bit foolish on several plays. But no one seems to jeer. It's a pleasant crowd that sees a good game. And most of them stay for the postgame fireworks.

By the time Sunday's game is over, there's talk that just maybe the White Sox can get back into playoff contention. It takes more than three hours to play longer than it should, perhaps, but the pitching is strong on both teams and the strategy is intriguing. The Sox win, 3-2.

Robin Ventura hits the game-winner, a single into center field, in the eighth after the batter ahead of him, Thomas, is intentionally walked. For much of the season, pitching around Thomas has worked fine, but not today. Scott Radinsky, who missed all of last season because of Hodgkin's disease, pitches the ninth inning for the save, his first since August of 1993. Oh, and Kruk, who's becoming another favorite of the fans of his new team, gets another hit.

Attendance is 27,514. Above the season average, again. When it's over, there's a delightful breeze off nearby Lake Michigan, and Robert Johnson's blues classic "Sweet Home, Chicago" is blaring on the stadium loudspeakers. At the moment, it's hard to imagine a more pleasant way to spend a summer Sunday than in the box seats in right field.

WRIGLEY FIELD, CHICAGO, JUNE 26

This is the purists' other old baseball shrine besides Fenway Park. And like Fenway, fans have flooded here for years to put up with some truly bad teams. This is yet another big-market franchise that is seemingly invulnerable to all these baseball crises you so often hear about and read about. The Cubs put together an eighth-inning rally but still lose, 8-6, to the dreadful Pittsburgh Pirates, a small-market team that might well have to move to simply survive. We're in our best seats yet, about 15 rows behind home plate, and shaking our heads over the Pirates' roster. Player after player no-names. Questions along the lines of "who is this guy?" bring more blank stares than anything else.

The rain that had seemed so ominous never comes, though, and it's another nice night at an old ball yard that until 10 years ago only had day games. Attendance is 21,967, a bit below average this year for the Cubs and baseball in general. Still, on a Monday night, Wrigley Field is like a magnet.

Six games in nine days. Yeah, I still like baseball. But no, it's not indispensable. Not to me. Not to anyone.

A few weeks later, I'm left with several contrasting memories. There was Naehring's homer in Boston that brought the crowd alive. Another potential star is emerging at Fenway. Then there was the sheer joy of watching Kruk, the very essence of a ballplayer. But then there were the two in-line skaters zipping down Brookline Avenue in Boston a couple of hours after a game, passing by Fenway like it just didn't matter. And finally, there was the guy in the ticket booth at Wrigley. I asked him what it was like this summer, the summer when baseball's supposed to be doomed, up on the North Side?

"Baseball or no baseball," he said, "there is always something going on."

Stanford's Band of Cruel Fools

San Francisco Examiner opinion piece, October 15, 1997

"Seamus O'Hungry," whose "sparse cultural heritage consisted only of fighting, then starving"—that's supposed to be witty?

Let's strike up the band—yes, the Stanford band again—for lessons in:

1. A deficiency in the history curriculum.

2. A disturbing pick-and-choose approach to political and ethnic sensibilities at what's supposed to be one of the top schools in the country.

Some kids at Stanford, in the band and in the audience, evidently found something funny about the Great Famine in Ireland 150 years ago. Funny enough to be the theme of Leland Stanford Junior University Marching Band's pregame and half-time shows October 4 for an intercollegiate football game against the Fighting Irish—get it?—of the University of Notre Dame.

Afterward, the band manager was quoted as saying that anyone who objected was overreacting. The university, admitting that grown-ups in the athletic department hadn't noticed anything wrong in an advance review of the script, issued a perfunctory apology and announced a wrist-slap punishment: Future Notre Dame games are off-limits to the band.

I was at the game, and I was appalled. And no, I'm not easily offended. I work in the newspaper business. I went to college once and engaged in my share of spoofs and mockery.

But I don't find anything funny about the famine that ravaged and killed more than a million people between 1845 and 1850. At least another million people fled Ireland, often for the United States and places like San Francisco.

Seems to me that the standards for satire get quite high when the target is the nation of Jonathan Swift, George Bernard Shaw, and Oliver St. John Gogarty.

Maybe the fools cheering for the band's program could brush up on current events. It was just a few months ago that the Brits came clean and acknowledged that the famine, far from being a laughing matter, was a human tragedy that London allowed to happen.

I left Stanford Stadium wondering where the ignorance of these kids ended and where their values began.

There's clearly something that the Stanford kids are missing, and I frankly wonder if that would be the case if more of them had been educated first in New York. There's a law in this state that says that the mass starvation in Ireland— many of us regard it as genocide—be part of the public school curriculum on human rights.

Perhaps it was a coincidence, but nine days after the Stanford performance, similar legislation was signed by Governor Wilson.

If I had a kid off at some pricey college who thought the Irish famine was something to laugh about rather than learn about, I'd put a stop to the tuition checks.

Sox Appeal

Times Union, Travel, June 20, 2004

Fenway may be sold out, but tickets were easy to acquire in St. Petersburg, Florida

St. Petersburg, Florida—The temperature has climbed above 90 when the plane touches down on a hazy day in late May for an oddly timed holiday in a surprisingly pleasant city. Back home, the weather is finally showing early traces of an upstate summer. Here, it's just the right occasion for the other guy in the airport shuttle van in from Arizona to see his mother and attend his 50th high school reunion to wax about the days when segregation was more common than air conditioning.

This is a trip dictated by the baseball schedule. Florida has major league ball now, not that Joe Bruno Stadium low minors stuff. And with spring training two months in the past, these games in Florida, not so long ago limited to Grapefruit League competition, truly matter.

Of course, baseball matters up north, too. In Boston, it matters too much: With the Red Sox virtually sold out at Fenway Park for the entire season, a plane ticket to St. Petersburg starts to make some sort of sense. What the *New Yorker*'s Roger Angell calls the "Bijou of Baseball" is overextended and overbooked. Time for a road trip.

Tropicana Field, the dreary, antiseptic downtown dome where the Tampa Bay Devil Rays play, is much more alive than usual. A crowd of almost 14,000 is on hand. Outside, a "scalper" is happy to sell tickets for face value, rather than taking a bath. Forty bucks lands a $40 ticket just past first base and only a few rows from the field, artificial grass and all. The same ticket would be almost twice as much at Fenway, for all its congested charm.

RED SOX NATION

I'm not the only one with the bright idea to head south. Inside, it's almost like a home game for what's known as the Red Sox Nation, which seems to make up about half of this sparse crowd.

Team regalia is the norm. Shirts with the names "Schilling" and "Martinez" on the back, for the Sox star pitchers; "Ramirez" the slugger; and "Garciaparra" for the then-ailing shortstop. And that's just in the seats and the clean, orderly concession lines.

A few blocks away, at Ferg's sports bar on Central Avenue, an older, weathered-looking fellow wears a Sox jersey bearing the word that's been with the tortured franchise for too many years of heartache: "Believe."

Sox fans are here from all over, not only in dress but in the accent and attitude that's all too obvious to a trained eye and ear. Had they not made their own trek to the Trop, they could have jammed the phone lines to those sports call-in shows back in New England.

Sean, from Tampa by way of Camden, Maine, is among the mellow ones. He's a former Down East fisherman who headed to Florida years ago for warmer weather and steadier work. The Sox are the draw for him, even as he encourages his young son to stick by the hometown 'Rays. When the Sox win, and the kid goes home with a foul ball his dad snagged, it seems like a nice night for both of them.

It's the more typically hard-core Sox fans, like Ed, from Orlando by way of Meriden, Connecticut, who bring a Boston feel to a game in an indoor stadium that's just a quarter full. Ed displays a chops-bustin' possessive streak toward two seats just a few rows behind the Sox dugout that are still empty in the fifth inning. He insists Curt Schilling, cruising along toward a fifth win of the season as he gives up just five hits, is struggling, even when no one else seems to agree. Ed wonders if Keith Foulke, an impressive off-season acquisition of a relief pitcher who saves another game for Boston, isn't overrated. He has an authoritative-sounding opinion about everything.

I take an instant liking to Ed. This is like being at Fenway, except with leg room, climate control (72, all the time), better food, and cleaner bathrooms.

NIGHTLIFE

We part, with this-is-the-yeaahh assurances, but without following his recommendations for late-night activity. That would have been Ibor City, about a $30 to $40 cab ride across the bay into Tampa. It's a section of the city with bar after bar that I'm later more reliably told resembles a redneck version of New Orleans's French Quarter.

Even Ferg's seems a bit on the wild side. Loud and crowded, it's said to be the sort of place where women will lift their skirts out of sheer spontaneity. This night, at least, there's a steady vibe of a scuffle just on the verge of breaking out. If it had, I suppose I could have hung close to the guy with the "Believe" shirt, who surely looks like he can take care of himself. Then, again, how good can his karma be?

The better place to wind down, I thought, was at a delightful jazz bar and restaurant called 10 Beach Drive (named after its address) in the basement of the funky-looking Ponce de Leon hotel. It's just east of the downtown, close to the bay and the city pier, and a part of St. Petersburg full of new construction and outright charm. The bay breeze, along with a humidity that's relented a bit, make for the sort of pleasant night and Southern flavor that keep the tourists coming.

When Tampa Bay got a major league team in 1999, there was talk that baseball, and especially the downtown stadium, was what St. Petersburg in particular needed. After Opening Day that year, the trite and boosterish headline on Page 1 of the otherwise well-respected St. Petersburg Times read "Rays' Defeat Can't Dampen Winning Spirit." Six years later, signs are everywhere that this isn't about to become a real baseball town. The franchise is struggling. The city seems nice enough without an outbreak of pennant fever.

BACK AT THE BALLGAME

Tropicana Field beckons the next night just as the outdoor temperature is down to a comfortable 81. In the press box and throughout the dome, hockey, of all things, commands as much attention as baseball. The Tampa Bay Lightning Bolts lose Game 6 of their semifinal series with the Philadelphia Flyers. (Still, they go on a month later to win the Stanley Cup.)

The 'Rays win one, though, much to the relief of an agitated manager, Lou Pinella. They unload on Boston pitcher Derek Lowe, who's struggling this season, just two years after he was a contender for the Cy Young award.

For some from the Sox nation, that means the night's a bust. It is, certainly, for Ed from Jacksonville, Florida, by way of the Boston suburb of Braintree, Massachusetts. "Look, all I wanna know the only thing I wanna know is what's Lowe's ERA now," he demands in a tone that suggests wicked high volume on the sports call-in shows and perhaps too much caffeine.

For the record, Lowe's ERA was 6.02 at that point, and it's not much better now. But Ed needs to do what everyone else in town, aside from the worst of the Red Sox lot, seems to be so adept at. Ed needs to take it more in stride.

He needs a day at nearby Fort De Soto Beach, for instance. It's the Gulf of Mexico, Ed, not the domed stadium a few miles to the east. All summer long, through Labor Day and past it, Sox fans will fret about their team at the grand beaches of New England. Few, if any, of them will be any nicer, though, than Fort De Soto, with its greenish-blue water and spectacular presence of seasonal and mildly exotic birds.

He needs a good dinner, too, of course. At the downtown Oyster Bar, not far from the stadium and closer still to Ferg's, he can go through three courses of raw oysters, tuna steak slices, and stuffed oysters without draining his travel funds. And every time, a bartender/waiter who looks like Johnny Cash will tell him what a good choice he just made.

Do all that, even if he didn't get around to visiting the Salvador Dalí museum, and he'll want to go back to St. Petersburg, when the Red Sox are in town or maybe when they're not. I know I do.

Thanks for the Memories

Times Union editorial, February 20, 1999

Was there anyone, anyone at all, on that great New York Yankees team last season who played the position of Everyman better than David Wells? Who could the folks drinking beer in the not-as-expensive-as-the-rest seats better identify with?

Here was this guy, well on the way to middle age, with off-the-field interests that ran toward barrooms, Harleys, and heavy metal music. And last summer, it was like he caught lightning in a bottle. There was the perfect game against the Minnesota Twins in May. There was the game against the Cleveland Indians in September when it looked as if he might do it again. As it was, the first 20 batters to face Mr. Wells went down. When it was over, he had a two-hit shutout, one more terrific ballgame on the way to an 18-4 season. In the playoffs, he was perfect again, 4-0.

And what does he get for it? A ticket to Toronto. A spot on the roster of a team that will struggle just to compete.

"It's a little emotional, you know?" he said shortly after getting the news. Who could phrase it better?

By trading Mr. Wells to the Blue Jays for Roger Clemens, the five-time Cy Young Award winner, the Yankees get a much better pitcher—on paper. But what about heart? What about fitting in so magnificently on a championship team that wasn't surly, like the Yankees of the Billy Martin and Reggie Jackson day? If last season in the Bronx was about the pure joy of baseball, it was largely due to Mr. Wells.

"We lost a little character today," said fellow pitcher David Cone, in the rhetorical equivalent of an off-speed pitch. "There are probably some establishments in Manhattan that will be down in the dumps today when they hear the news. There may be some bars going out of business," he added, with a dead-on delivery.

Even with Mr. Clemens in the rotation, can next year's Yankees possibly be better than, or even as good as, last year's team?

If things go astray, even for just a few games, the fans who pay too much for tickets and even cable TV might well turn on George Steinbrenner, the owner who can't be satisfied. And when they're ticked off at Mr. Steinbrenner, when they seethe that he hardly has their interests in mind, they'll be closer than ever to their man, to their Everyman, David Wells.

How 'Bout Those Sawx?

Times Union editorial, October 22, 2004

Even today, more than 24 hours later, there still might well be people in New England and here on the western fringe of Red Sox Nation who think their ball club just won the World Series. Somewhere on a fancy college campus, or in a dumpy old mill town, along the seacoast or on a mountaintop, in an unaffordable suburb or in a dingy housing project, there might even be fans who think that coming from three games behind and beating the hated New York Yankees to win the American League pennant is better than winning the World Series.

Understand, they're not delirious. They're merely getting ahead of themselves.

Overcoming the Yankees is a cleansing experience for all those generations of Red Sox faithful for whom disappointment has been like oxygen, mother's milk, and bitter fruit—all at once. The ancient menaces of Harry Frazee and Babe Ruth aren't quite vanquished. Not just yet. But neither do they loom nearly so large.

Wow, that was some baseball that was played over in Fenway Park and down at Yankee Stadium. The greatest comeback in baseball history. That much, you'll always be able to look up.

Was anyone ever as tough as the injured Curt Schilling, sucking it up to win Game 6? And when was the last time someone was as due, as they say, as Johnny Damon, busting out of a playoff slump to hit two home runs in Game 7?

Was there anyone as gracious and stoic in defeat as Yankees manager Joe Torre, the statesman of baseball?

This one needs to be savored, even with the first pitch of the World Series scheduled for only about 36 hours from now. To appreciate the beauty of the Boston triumph, and the drama of upsetting New York, though, it might actually help to be a more dispassionate fan. Or even not much of a baseball fan at all.

To be a Red Sox die-hard, though, meant taking Thursday night only partially off. There was the decisive game of the St. Louis Cardinals–Houston Astros National League pennant series to watch. There was a World Series opponent to be scouted.

True, unadulterated victory is four games off. It's still been since 1918 since Boston won it all.

The saying goes back there, credited to the *Boston Globe*'s John Powers, that the bar stools are full of people who led the Boston Marathon in Ashland, about five miles into a 26-mile race. Beating the Yankees can't be dismissed that readily. It is, instead, like leading the marathon in Kenmore Square, by Fenway Park, about 24 or so miles deep.

It feels that good for Sox fans, with the finish line oh, so close.

Editors' note: The Red Sox went on to defeat the St. Louis Cardinals in the 2004 World Series, ending an 86-year streak without a World Series championship. The Red Sox also won the World Series in 2007, over the Florida Marlins, and in 2013, once again defeating the Cardinals, five weeks after Jim's death.

Why Didn't He Do More?

Times Union editorial, November 10, 2011

If only this were merely about football. Or about ham-handed communications and bureaucratic bungling at some far-off university. Instead, it involves one of the most grotesque crimes imaginable—the sexual abuse of children—and the breach of trust and power that keeps those crimes from being properly investigated.

Coach Joe Paterno is being forced into retirement at Penn State. That might well make the elder statesman of college football, until last week revered across Pennsylvania and beyond it, the most prominent casualty of a sexual abuse scandal since Cardinal Bernard Law resigned in Boston in 2002.

Pedophilia, in all its ugliness and all its tragedy, has again captured the public's rapt attention. And it's because someone in a position of such unquestioned authority didn't take it seriously enough.

It does little for Mr. Paterno's reputation, and far less for the apparent victims of his one-time heir apparent Jerry Sandusky, that he seems to have satisfied his legal obligation by reporting the alleged rape of a young boy at the Penn State football complex in 2002 to his boss, then-athletic director Tim Curley—who resigned and was indicted this week.

The law is clearly inadequate. In Pennsylvania, it is the responsibility of "the person in charge of the school or institution" to contact child welfare authorities in cases like this one. That absolves Mr. Paterno too readily.

Even in New York, where what are known as mandatory reporting laws still aren't rigorous enough, someone in Mr. Paterno's position would have been required to go to the police.

Then, of course, there's the moral obligation of Mr. Paterno and anyone else in a position like his, however uncomfortable it might be. At Penn State, the roster of enablers, as detailed by legal authorities, extends from the once-distinguished coach to all-but-anonymous university employees.

One apparent victim's anguish led to another's, Pennsylvania authorities say, both before Mr. Paterno became aware of the allegations against Mr. Sandusky and after he did.

"Nothing happened. Nothing stopped," says state police commissioner Frank Noonan, even after Mr. Sandusky first acknowledged to campus police in 1998 that he had engaged in improper behavior with young boys in the shower room.

Finally, with Mr. Sandusky facing a 40-count criminal indictment that could land him in prison for seven years, the rest of us can take stock of the latest sordid case of the most innocent people imaginable allegedly brutalized by people they trusted.

For Mr. Paterno, that means something sadly close to banishment.

"This is a tragedy. It is one of the great sorrows of my life," he said in a statement released Wednesday. "With the benefit of hindsight, I wish I had done more."

If that's not a piercing cry for a society more vigilant about the sexual abuse of minors, complete with stronger reporting laws, nothing is.

I'LL BE HOME

Jim, far right, in his final year at Boston Latin School, with a group of his Boston Latin soccer teammates in the fall of 1974. They were on their way to a soccer match at Magazine Beach Field in Cambridge. This photograph was taken about a half block from Commonwealth Avenue, near Boston University, on the boundary between the Allston section of Boston and the adjacent town of Brookline. Photograph by E. F. X. Cusack.

Introduction

A Man at Last at Peace with Himself

Darryl McGrath

My husband, Jim McGrath—and it was always "Jim," never "James," in his byline
and even on the *Times Union* masthead—considered newspaper journalism his true
church.

He was a lapsed Boston Irish Catholic, who left Catholicism far behind in
early adulthood with a dismissive, biting scorn. But he kept the essentials of his
Catholic beliefs, which in turn fueled his compassionate approach to the human
foibles about which he wrote. Jim's early inculcation into a deeply flawed but also
deeply humane faith, paradoxically, formed the basis for his approach to journalism.

He drew on those inner guidelines to truly give a voice to the voiceless—an
old adage that nevertheless says it best about Jim's writing. His words conveyed
beauty, passion, indignation, empathy, outrage, humor, and, ultimately, love. Love
for his craft and also for the characters, both tragic and sympathetic, who populated his writing. He expressed anger at the frequent unfairness of life better than
anyone I knew. But he also expressed humor and tenderness better than any writer
I have ever read, because he knew that those qualities acted as necessary counter-
weights to anger.

The title of this section, "I'll Be Home," comes from a book proposal that Jim
wrote for a fellowship application. He didn't get the fellowship. But the title for
a book that would have been an ode to the blue-collar Boston neighborhood of
his birth aptly describes the pieces in this section, which are all really about Jim's
strong yearning for a sense of place in his life. He was orphaned in college. His
father died first of a heart attack; his mother, nine months later, in a car accident;
and the summer that Jim turned 20 was the last that he spent in his parents' home.
Having a home mattered to Jim, more than most people realized.

These eight deeply personal pieces include Jim's profile of his father, a newspaper printer broken by a series of crippling strikes in Boston in the 1970s, but
whom Jim remembered as the man who always marked Jim's birthday with a card
printed from typeface that spelled out Jim's name, like a miniature newspaper,
which his father had fashioned for him the night before in the pressroom. His brief
but powerful recollection of the first Christmas he spent with his family after the

deaths of his parents, in "A Road to New Hampshire," is so evocative that the reader can sense the silence that follows a snowfall on a quiet Christmas morning.

This section also includes Jim's account of his visit to the grave of the Capital Region's first soldier to die in Afghanistan. His elegiac essays for the University of Michigan and Norman Mailer Writers Colony journalism fellowships describe his formative Brighton upbringing, as does his reflection on the arrest of Boston mobster and murderer Whitey Bulger. His love for Albany comes through in his farewell to the pay phone in his favorite bar. His account of a trip to Cooperstown in July 2013, for a wedding, evokes a special adolescent memory—a vacation with his best friend's family.

The Cooperstown essay was Jim's last piece to be published during his life, on August 30, 2013. He died five days later. The *Times Union* would publish one final bylined piece from Jim, in December 2013. That was a tribute to Nelson Mandela, written in the summer when Mandela's death seemed imminent, and then held until Mandela did die, with an editor's note explaining the posthumous publication.

But I love the fact that the Cooperstown piece, with its sweet note of optimism and joy, was the last of Jim's writing to be published in his lifetime. It reads like something written by a man at peace with himself and his life, who had achieved the sense of place that he sought, who had found a home, in Albany, and that is how I hope all of Jim's many readers will best remember him.

Darryl McGrath is an Albany author and journalist. She and Jim met at the *Times Union* in 1996 and married in 2001. They made their home in downtown Albany, where Darryl still lives.

Somebody's Thinking of Charlie McGrath

Times Union opinion piece, June 20, 1993

I shall think of my father today, not because it's Father's Day, which he really didn't like to begin with, but because I think of him almost every day, at odd times and in ways that I don't necessarily expect you to understand.

His name was Charlie McGrath. He died 16 years ago, when he had a wife and family, had just bought a house in the suburbs, and was looking ahead to a very uncertain future.

He worked at a newspaper, just like I do. I'm often struck by just how similar our work patterns are, especially when you consider just how different we are in so many other ways. But he went to work when I do, when most people are coming home and getting ready for supper. He came home, as I do, well after midnight to a routine I often follow—spread the paper out on the kitchen table, read it over a few beers, and try not wake anyone else up—one of the many things he did better than I do.

What else can I tell you about him?

He grew up in a working-class neighborhood of Boston called Brighton in the same two-family house his father had lived in. He was in the Navy in World War II and he had a trade. He was a newspaper printer. Perhaps more than anything else, that defines the way I recall him.

Now you have to understand there was nothing fancy about Brighton during the 60s and 70s. On one side of us lived a man named Reilly, a detective with the Boston police, and his family. He was an ugly racist. His youngest son was the person whose name I got in response the first time I asked what a juvenile delinquent was.

On the other side of us was the Brass family. Brass was a special delivery mailman. He was a prince of a guy who took the kids on the street for ice cream, to ballgames, and to amusement parks. He drank a lot, too, and actually took pride in defying the stereotype that Jewish people aren't heavy drinkers, not like the Irish. Mrs. Brass is a much respected and liked nurse at a Boston hospital and still lives on our street.

There was a family named Caniglia. They emigrated from Italy by way of Argentina and were factory workers. Their son was one of my best friends and played soccer for my team's archrival. And there was the Szocik family. The mother worked in a garment factory and hosted huge parties every Easter.

Later, there were more and more Asian American families: the Moys, the Ngs, the Yongs. They owned their own businesses and seemed to live a bit better than we did.

There were no doctors, lawyers, bankers, or even teachers that I can remember on our street.

Living in that environment, I thought for a time my father had one of the most important jobs anyone could have. He went to work at night, on weekends, and sometimes even on Christmas Eve and Christmas.

Every morning, an early-edition copy of the *Herald* or the *Record-American*, depending on where my father was working at the time, would be on the kitchen table. By the time I got to school in the morning, I had seen the paper, especially the box scores. It made me feel important.

Sometimes the easiest way to remember things isn't by how old I was, or what grade I was in, but by what turmoil was going on in the Boston newspaper trade and how it hit home. I recall, for instance, a strike in the 1960s, when every Sunday for what seems like a couple of months we ate supper at the Burger King on Brighton Avenue. I remember 1967, when the most important thing to me was the Red Sox and the American League pennant race, but the main topic of conversation at the supper table was the fate of a dying afternoon paper called the *Boston Traveller*. My father was working for the sister paper, the morning *Herald*, at the time, but if the *Traveller* went under, his job would be in jeopardy.

The *Traveller* did go out of business that year. We were driving to Cape Cod for a few days of vacation when we heard on the radio that the paper was finished.

That meant my father no longer had a permanent "situation." So he'd leave the house each night and stop by what then was known as the *Herald-Traveller*, then maybe the *Record American* or the *Globe*, present his union card and try to get hired as a substitute for the night. It worked—usually—but meant no regular days off or paid vacations. Sometimes there was no work, and my father would return home defeated.

It was around then—I was about 12 or 13—that I realized my father absolutely hated the newspaper business. He saw it mostly through the perspective of his own trade. It was dying, and the pay wasn't getting any better. He thought the publishers were greedy, and he saw the unions, especially his own, as unable to do much to salvage his livelihood. I began to notice how much it seemed to pain him as he rushed out of the house after supper to go off and make the only living he thought he could.

Perhaps it's just coincidence, but the only Father's Day I really remember has a link to the newspaper business. It was in 1972, the day the *Herald-Traveller* published its last edition. It was merging with the *Record American*. There would only be two papers in Boston, and every printer lost a bit more job security.

So things were tense around the house. My brother and his wife were visiting, and it was quite festive the night before, with lots of food and even more beer. The next day gave way to a more anxious mood, and it probably didn't help that I was getting ready to go on a bike trip to Canada that no one wanted me to go on. As my brother and sister-in-law were leaving, Mimi, who hadn't known my father very long, told him she was sorry it wasn't much of a Father's Day.

He responded as directly as I can ever remember him doing, saying in effect he was a father 365 days a year and Father's Day was a gimmick cooked up by the greeting card industry.

These are the things I think about, almost every day.

The events of his life don't change, of course, but my own perspective does. I have worked in the newspaper business, the business he hated, since I got out of college 14 years ago. It's different, I realize, because he was a printer and I'm an editor, and I like what I do. I also have worked, at last count anyway, for two papers that no longer exist.

I sometimes find other people, my own newspaper contemporaries mostly, are especially curious that my father was a printer, and what relevance that might have to what I do. My father encouraged my interest in the newspaper business in part, I'm sure, as a sort of damage control against my fulfilling his worst fears and being an underachiever.

I remember two things about the last time I talked with him from a pay phone in the lobby of a college dorm halfway across the country. He had just found out the *Herald American* was laying off him and a bunch of other printers. He joked about maybe buying a fishing boat but was worried the best he'd do would be to land a job as a security guard. The other thing I remember telling him is I was going to be the editor of the college paper. He was happy to hear that and suggested that maybe I could get a summer job working in the newsroom at one of the local papers.

Charlie McGrath is buried, next to my mother, in a simple veterans' cemetery in Scituate, Massachusetts, about 30 miles south of Boston. There are no headstones, just two small plaques on the ground. The one over my father's grave says he served in the Navy. At least that's the way I remember it. I haven't been there in 14 years. I don't need to go, really. The newspaper business, with its frustrations, uncertainties, and for me, at least, rewards—with its nights, holidays, and weekends—sustains the bond between us. It's enough to make me think about him, almost every day.

Happy Father's Day.

A Road to New Hampshire

Times Union, Life and Leisure, December 25, 1994

Christmas, I'm convinced, is about expectations more than anything else, starting with a small kid's lofty hopes for what might be under the tree.

By the time I was 21 and a senior in college, the expectations for Christmas were awfully low. My mother had died two days prior to Christmas the year before, the same year my father died, and none of us were looking forward to the holidays.

So four of us—one of my brothers, his wife, my sister, and I (we were sort of a rump family unit at that point, at least for the holidays)—headed off to hang out for a few days in a part of New Hampshire where I had never been.

The idea was to get away from everything, from the pageantry to the memories.

I often think about that trip and our time together. It was 16 years ago; I remember that we went cross-country skiing. I remember that vividly. I vaguely remember that we went to see a dreadful Ryan O'Neal movie in a theater on the main street in Hanover. We had a nice dinner on Christmas Eve, across the river in Vermont. I remember that, too.

What I especially remember, though, is Christmas Day. It had snowed heavily overnight, and you pretty much needed four-wheel drive just to get around. Everything in Hanover seemed to be closed, so we piled into my brother's Toyota Land Cruiser and headed north on Route 87 into Vermont again.

There were hardly any cars on the road. We talked a bit, looked at the passing countryside, and listened to some tapes on a tinny-sounding car stereo. Mostly, though, we just drove.

We finally got off the highway in some town in Vermont—I can't remember the name of it—and found a general store that was open. We picked up some beer and newspapers, and some crackers and cheese, and headed back toward Hanover.

The sun was out by then, and I remember thinking that it really was a great New England winter day. And for all the low expectations, it was a good Christmas, too: quiet, peaceful, and delightfully uneventful.

Soldiering On

Another Generation, Another War,
Another Cause to Honor and Remember

Times Union opinion piece, May 26, 2002

Pile the bodies high at Austerlitz and Waterloo.
Shovel them under and let me work.—
                    I am the grass; I cover all.

And pile them high at Gettysburg
And pile them high at Ypres and Verdun.
Shovel them under and let me work.
Two years, ten years, and the passengers ask the conductor:
                    "What place is this?
                    Where are we now?"

                    I am the grass.
                    Let me work.
                    —Carl Sandburg, "Grass"

Where are we indeed?

US Army Sergeant 1st Class Daniel Petithory's grass is at the bottom of a slightly sloping hill in a cemetery in Cheshire, Massachusetts, snug inside the Berkshire mountains. A small wooden cross, surrounded by a half dozen or so tiny American flags and a Green Beret teddy bear in a secure plastic bag, among other paraphernalia, mark the place of burial for one of the early, and still one of the relatively few, American casualties of the war in Afghanistan.

This is where the kid who joined the service right out of the local high school 15 years ago, just as he vowed, has come home at age 32.

And this is where we are, then, too. This is where war, one after another, brings us. To the grave sites of all it's claimed, where it seems everyone knows the kid, and then the man, who dreamed of being a soldier, but wasn't supposed to die.

To make the rounds of a quaint and rural place like Cheshire, population 3,600, a few miles, two towns, and one shopping mall past the gasping city of Pittsfield, is to come painfully close to the soldier and the civilian both. Those are real lives, or were, under Sergeant Petithory's grass and under Carl Sandburg's grass, that landscape that extends, well, forever.

At the gas station/convenience store on Route 8, the distracted-looking kid stocking the shelves comes fully alert at the mention of Sergeant Petithory. The directions to Cheshire Cemetery are flawless.

"Oh, it would be over there," a woman says solemnly at the cemetery itself, pointing past the road that splits a grassy stretch of, at most, a few hundred graves.

"Too young," a man says, back in town to attend to another grave site, but eager to find the grave of a Special Forces sergeant killed last December north of Kandahar, where Afghan opposition forces overcame the last stand of the Taliban. Killed, that is, by a bomb carrying 2,000 pounds of explosives after an American B-52 missed its target.

"Too young," he repeats, before explaining that his mother knew Sergeant Petithory's mother, and not needing to explain his own need to be here. And so this fellow, paunchy and balding, of the Vietnam generation, probably, carefully makes his way down the damp hill to Sergeant Petithory's grave.

A few strides short of that special ground, he stops and salutes. Nothing forced, it appears, and hardly self-conscious. A simple salute to a man not much more than half his age.

This is Memorial Day in the New England countryside. This is Memorial Day across the land.

It is Carl Sandburg's America, where Daniel Petithory rests. It's the America that's been to war before. The America that went to war, the Great War, in the poet's day to make the world safe for democracy. The America that now fights a war against terror, one that may transcend all the others.

It's the grass, though, that links all those wars together. It's just a few steps from Sergeant Petithory's grave to Pasquale Penna's grave. He fought in World War I, in Italy. He was lucky. He survived, and came home. He was 101 when they buried him here three years ago.

Then there's Giacomo Cozzaglio, a few rows over. He was a US Army private in the same war. Born in 1896, two years before Pasquale Penna. Died in 1984.

The next generation had its war. And here lies Peter Massitcani, an Army staff sergeant, 1914–1998.

Down in Pittsfield, Marine Private Frank Russell Whittlesey (1921–1942) is buried next to his parents. Only they were there first. Private Whittlesey was killed in the jungles of Guadalcanal, attending to a wounded buddy as enemy soldiers closed in. His remains weren't found until a farmer dug them up, by accident, in 1989. He was reburied on Memorial Day in 1992, with taps and a 12-shot salute from M-16 rifles, fired by his fellow Marines. A farewell not unlike that extended in December to Sergeant Petithory.

Wartime soldiers all.

It's time again to walk down all those hills, over all that damp grass, to honor them simply by remembering them.

And to ask, when do the wars end?

"Journeys Like Mine Should Never Really End"

The world where I'm from, in the Brighton neighborhood of Boston, would fit naturally and snugly enough into any good history of postwar America. The people had jobs, not careers. They owned houses, if they were lucky, usually two-families or three-deckers, not property. They accepted, even supported, a certain social order. They didn't necessarily aspire to be rich, and would have been uncomfortable at the very idea of being important. But neither were they willing to be screwed. That much, they only even warily suspected. For that, they had come too far.

These people were cops and firemen, nurses and school teachers, social workers and government clerks, contractors and factory workers, and, in my father's case, a newspaper printer. And, of course, there was the ill-placed accountant, the struggling but married graduate student, a judge whose connections aroused a certain suspicion, a rabbi, and a professor at a small Catholic women's college.

They had stories to tell, surely, but not necessarily intellectual biographies to mention. In my own house there were hopes and indeed expectations. Achievement and mobility were distant, but not unwelcome, words. Intellect was a different, and slightly threatening, concept. It was a place of few books, aside from a set of supermarket-purchased encyclopedias so outdated that they featured President Eisenhower's picture.

Still, these people read—newspapers mostly, in a time, three and four decades ago, when that was really the only place to turn for the information they sought. Remember, they accepted the social order and did more than they probably realized to reinforce it. But they had expectations in return.

Corruption and malfeasance were ever present, from the Boston school system all the way to the White House and Watergate. It was only the level of monetary greed that perhaps couldn't keep pace with the generations of scandal ahead.

That's the world I grew up in, not at all unlike the one across the river in Cambridge, where Jimmy Breslin wrote of Tip O'Neill and the people who didn't go to Harvard in his 1975 book, *How the Good Guys Finally Won: Notes from an Impeachment Summer*. And that's pretty much the world where I first became a journalist almost 30 years ago. Thinking back, it was a sort of high tide for newspapers. The traditional mission of demanding accountability from those in power was well intact, then, in the late 1970s. The gimmickry and silliness, the obsession with the celebrity culture, and the disregard for the more common citizen came soon enough.

I was lucky enough to catch the last days of a less complicated era for newspapers when I broke into this business. In 1979, just after graduating from nearby Lake Forest College, I was working for the *News-Sun*, in Waukegan, Illinois, along the Lake Michigan Rust Belt. It was a family-owned paper, by that of the journalist and author Ward Just. We covered politics and government, good guys and bad guys, stories of corruption and tales of hope quite aggressively for a relatively small paper. Or so it seems all these years later.

That was a journalism that well suited and well served the people in Waukegan but also back in Brighton. Only by 2006, nothing is quite the same, and no story so simple or uplifting, as a kid reporter's experiences three decades earlier. It's amazing enough that I was in Waukegan, armed with a notebook and the seemingly boundless curiosity that merged street smarts with the liberal arts education I obtained by leaving Brighton and going off to school at Lake Forest. The best I can do now is to remember the larger issues and lessons—indeed, the values—of those times. I think I have.

They're an almost vanishing species now, these people with jobs but not careers, who craved information but held suspicions of intellect, who were determined to advance with instincts more than books.

What they have now, as they always did, is a vague social contract of their own, without being able to pick John Locke out of their woefully outdated encyclopedias and without ever knowingly trusting the likes of the demagogic politicians who come along with dreary regularity. They deserve better, especially from their government.

I've been writing editorials for the Albany *Times Union* for about ten years or so now, and I hoped I've maintained the focus I'm here preaching about. I've written, for instance, about an inept and mean-spirited district attorney in nearby Rensselaer County who just last fall had the hubris, not to mention the support of the state Senate majority leader and the political machine he controls, to run for judge. My editorials helped keep this woman, Patricia DeAngelis, off the bench. She remains a county prosecutor, though, with a disregard for genuine justice that makes victims of the people unfortunate enough to wind up in court in the first place. Brighton was full of such people, lacking education and connections, whose lives could have been made all the worse by zealous prosecutors and inept judges.

I've written, too, about a political activist in Brooklyn whose life was all but ruined by a district attorney out to avenge his incessant challenges to the local Democratic political machine. John Kennedy O'Hara could have been me, or any other working-class resident of Brooklyn who dared to embrace a progressive agenda and become involved in politics.

To seek freedom from such injustice is an extreme, however realistic, case, of course. The people on the dependent end of that same social contract want, at times demand, and above all need decent public schools. Otherwise they descend from stakeholders to casualties of a system they so willingly accepted. In Brighton, and throughout Boston, in the 1960s and 1970s the schools were for the most part terrible. The politicians, Irish and Catholic mostly, who controlled the schools were far more interested in maintaining them as a haven of patronage jobs than they were in educating the children of the people who depended upon them. The citywide high schools where admission came via an entrance exam, including the one I attended, were the rare refuge from the system itself. Worse still was the zeal in which an especially rigid, even ruthless, form of de facto segregation was enforced. (J. Anthony Lukas explained it in exhaustive and masterful detail in his 1985 book, *Common Ground*.)

Albany's schools have suffered, too, and not so dissimilarly. I've written editorial after editorial in support and defense of the public school system here, and of the people who won't abandon it and of those who can't abandon it. The stakes are enormous. A collective vote of no confidence in the public schools will mean an exodus of the city's middle class.

In a city where aging school buildings were literally crumbling, my editorials were a driving force behind the passage of a series of referendums in 2001 and again in 2003 that financed a $185 million city school construction and renovation plan. Everything from my own reporting to anecdotal evidence to pure instinct tells me that the *Times Union* editorial page has helped keep families in the city when the pressure and temptation to leave is constant.

Quite often our advocacy for the Albany schools puts us at odds with an aggressive mayor, himself a former high school assistant principal, whose otherwise strong vision for the city includes a troubling desire to take over the schools. There are days when I feel like I'm reliving my Boston years, when I was forever reading the *Boston Globe* as its editorial writers and columnists clashed with politicians on school issues there.

Anything I write about Albany, about schools or crime or taxes or just the challenges and satisfaction of living here, is to further embrace a sense of place. It's a notion that's too often missing in American newspapers, especially when nearly all the papers are owned by large, out-of-town corporations. Reporters and editors and the rest are their own constituents. In one sense, I left Brighton, went to college and graduate school, and have had a series of jobs a lot closer to the careers that eluded those people. But in another sense, I've replaced Brighton for Albany, where I live, admittedly, in a nicer house full of all the books we didn't have. At 48, I'm likely to finish my working years here, experiencing the conditions and consequences I write about, reaping what I sow.

I'm less of a spectator and more of a participant, surely. I write—and in an influential forum, yet—about what people in both Brighton and Albany might otherwise be inclined to talk about at their kitchen tables and on their front porches. What doesn't change are the values and expectations. It's as critical as ever that the people get a fair hearing in court, an honest and efficient government in exchange for their tax dollars and can send their kids to schools that aid social mobility, not prevent it.

Just as critical, but perhaps more obtuse, is the exposure to ideas. Intellect shouldn't be the least bit threatening. Journeys, like mine from Brighton to Albany, shouldn't ever really end. It's time to retrace, as much as I can, part of that journey.

It was just over 30 years ago when I went off to school in the Midwest, aided by federal as well as private financial aid programs, and encouraged by accommodating and accessible professors. The concept of intellect couldn't have been more welcoming. The world couldn't have seemed more inviting.

Truly, I can't imagine what would await a midcareer newspaperman at the University of Michigan. My hunch is that the world of ideas would be a more comfortable and enriching place than ever and the unending journey from Brighton to Albany would be more satisfying than ever.

Jim McGrath's 2006 autobiographical essay accompanied his application for a University of Michigan journalism fellowship.

"I'll Be Home"

Statement about My Work and My Goals

The world where I'm from, in the Brighton neighborhood of Boston, would fit naturally and snugly enough into any good history of postwar America. The people had jobs, not careers. They owned houses, if they were lucky, not property. They accepted, even supported, a certain social order. These people were cops and firemen, nurses and school teachers, social workers and government clerks, and, in my father's case, a newspaper printer.

They had stories to tell, surely, but not necessarily intellectual biographies to mention. That's the world I grew up in, and that's pretty much the world where I became a journalist 30 years ago. I've been writing editorials for the Albany *Times Union* for about 15 years or so now, and I hope I've maintained the focus I'm preaching about here.

Anything I write about Albany, about schools or crime or taxes or just the challenges and satisfaction of living here, is to further embrace a sense of place. I left Brighton when I went to college and graduate school. But in another sense, I've replaced Brighton for Albany, where I now live. That connection has given me the idea for a memoir, which in my mind I call, *I'll Be Home*.

I've long thought that the people I grew up with in Brighton—a doomed middle class, although they didn't think of themselves that way—and the characters I've known here in Albany in the bars, the bookstores, and from my own stoop—could figure into a collection of essays. The subjects would be those same people who lived—or live—in these old neighborhoods sometimes by choice, and sometimes by chance, but always with the same pride of place that I carried out of Brighton and into my world of a newspaperman's recollections.

I would benefit from some expert guidance, particularly on the question of whether this idea might be one book or two. Could I—should I—tell the bittersweet story from my youth of the bachelor party in the basement of an auto body shop near Harvard Stadium? Could that story exist in the same book as the tale of an Albany bar where you could see a couple on their first date just as easily as you could find yourself providing relationship advice to a young friend? I hope that a week at the Norman Mailer Writers Colony would help me begin to answer such questions.

Jim McGrath's 2011 application essay for the Norman Mailer Writers Colony residency.

A Vanishing Call of the Wild

Times Union opinion piece, August 10, 2009

I was hanging out on Madison Avenue, up the block from Lark Street, as the sun was beginning to go down the other night. It's a great time to indulge in what for my tastes is the best stretch of Albany for people-watching. There was the standard collection of workaday pedestrians, a good representation of hipsters, the usual bar flies, neighborhood regulars, a few recognizable eccentrics, an assortment of bicyclists and motorcyclists, a couple of cops on foot patrol, and quite a few dogs.

Yet all I could seem to do was stare at the pay phone by the bus stop at the corner of Lark.

My pay phone.

No, I'm not involved in any sort of unsavory business. Just journalism. But until last week, when I joined seemingly everyone else I know and acquired a cell phone, pay phones were where I made many of my calls.

As cell phones became ubiquitous, pay phones started to disappear. It was supply and demand, or maybe the other way around, right there on the streets. Nationally, there are fewer than half as many pay phones now than there were a dozen years ago. In the entire 518 area code, the count is down to barely 2,700 and, of course, shrinking. Among the casualties is the pay phone in Albany where I first called an acquaintance who soon enough became my wife.

One more piece of communal infrastructure is vanishing as we retreat into our personal and insular worlds. Anyone can scrape together two quarters, but can everyone afford a cell phone contract? And should they really have to do so?

Knowing where a working pay phone could reliably be found had become something between an odd hobby and an outright obsession with me. On the rare occasions when someone else was using the one at Lark and Madison, I felt almost as if I were being gracious in sharing it. Oh, and can you make it quick? I've got a call or two to make myself. No slamming down the receiver or scuffing up things, either, now.

That phone always works, too. It's a few blocks down the street, at Madison and Swan, that making a call is more of a crap shoot. The phone there doesn't seem to like nickels or dimes and frequently is on the blink altogether.

Back in the other direction, though, at New Scotland and Madison, there's a nice one that's been working again for a few years now. It even has volume control, and how rare that feature has become. Of course, your handle is an impersonal one on that phone. Having "City of Albany" show up on caller ID has a way of catching your friends off guard. It was across the street, at the pay phone outside what used to be Ralph's Tavern, that there was little mystery who was on the line.

Already one friend wonders if I will still make an occasional call from my favorite pay phones. And I just might, as a way to clear my conscience and help keep them in business. It reminds me of almost 20 years ago when a zillionaire from Mexico started a daily newspaper called the *National*, devoted solely to sports. Good as it was, with writers and editors from top newspapers and magazines, there were doubts from the get-go that it could stay in business. I bought it and read it every day. At the end, before it folded, I was buying two copies. You know, doing my part.

Next time I feel compelled to plunk a couple of quarters into a pay phone, I suppose I could call myself—on my cell.

Boston, the Bulgers, and Me

Times Union opinion piece, August 19, 2013

For a middle-aged Irish guy like me, who came of age in the working-class precincts and public schools of Boston, the most riveting news for months now has been back in what used to be home. Nothing in scandal-plagued Albany comes close.

It's in Boston where one of the most violently and ruthlessly venal people in the history of America, a once-fabled goon named Whitey Bulger, stood trial for a spree of murders that he carried out over more than two decades with the explicit sponsorship of the FBI. Whitey was found guilty last week of just about everything the feds could throw at him in a case that had the government itself on trial.

Boston is also where some of the most viciously false manufactured history imaginable, even in a city still haunted by the Irish attraction for delusional sentiment, exploded as well. The whole Bulger family has fallen further from grace and deeper into the black hole of condemnation.

Whitey has a brother, you see. Two, actually—including a disgraced political hack named Jackie, himself a convicted felon for trying to cover Whitey's tracks while he was on the run from 1994 to 2011. The other, more prominent brother is Billy, once the feared leader of the Massachusetts state Senate and later the president of the University of Massachusetts.

Now, Billy might as well be underground himself. The brother act, in which one further empowered the other, is over. Billy is a lot more than what his press clippings suggested for far too long—a charming and scholarly if hard-edged politician who had to endure a roguish but ultimately not so thoroughly dangerous gangster of an older brother.

Billy's downfall began first, actually. It was 10 years ago this summer—I wasted a day of a vacation on Cape Cod watching C-SPAN—that Billy got hauled before a congressional committee investigating the corruption of the FBI by using the likes of Whitey as a prosecution-free informant. Billy was pressed to explain himself, not as the latter-day Marcus Aurelius he fancied himself, but quite literally as his contemptible brother's keeper.

Billy told Congress where to go, that he felt no obligation to help bring Whitey into custody before he killed again. With that, he was done at UMass.

Some family, isn't it?

Jackie was a constant presence at Whitey's trial. But not Billy. He resurfaced, sort of, in a recent *Boston Globe* story in which he portrayed himself and what had come of his career as one more victim of Whitey's life of crime.

It's around this point in this appalling tale that I inevitably think of one of the most noble families I know. It's David Kaczynski; his wife, Linda Patrik; and his late mother, Wanda.

Their role in bringing Ted Kaczynski to justice for the carnage he committed as the Unabomber is well known around here, of course. Less so around Boston, however. I well recall making the moral comparisons in an email exchange with a suburban Boston newspaper columnist a decade ago. This guy, too, was of the unsettling opinion that Billy's obligation was to his brother, and not to any larger sense of justice.

Yet it's David's enduring honor and courage that sticks with me as the myths of the Bulgers lie in tatters.

Here was Billy in 1990, at the retirement dinner of John Connolly, Whitey's handler in the FBI and now in prison for his role in one of Whitey's murders.

Billy quoted the Roman philosopher Seneca: "Loyalty is the holiest good in the human heart."

Loyalty to whom, Billy? Loyalty to what?

Enough, already, of Seneca. Enough of the self-serving and self-deluding classicist act.

You can learn better lessons about loyalty—both legitimately directed and obscenely misplaced—from David Kaczynski, a man who's more humble and more wise than you'll ever be.

And then you can slink out of hiding and explain yourself.

Editors' note: Whitey Bulger was found beaten to death at the Hazelton federal prison in West Virginia October 30, 2018, shortly after his arrival there. He was 89. Other inmates were suspected in his killing.

Small Town's Appeal Crosses Generations

Cooperstown Sparks Musings on the Past and the Future

Times Union, Living, August 30, 2013

The Schoharie Valley looks just the way it always does, and always should, on yet another summer trip to Cooperstown. There are the small-town centers that strike me as so pastorally American, and maybe even more vibrant than they actually are, on the drive out Route 20.

The slightly rolling hills off in the western distance are as impressive as ever. Closer to town, there's the ever-inviting, landscape-changing sight of Otsego Lake, and later the cottages and motels that could make these seasonal visits last much longer.

My wife, Darryl, is doing the driving. Just as well, since our friend Pete and I are taking in all the very different scenery and pleasant vibe that's so disarmingly close to Albany. Finally, there's the Fenimore Art Museum right there to the east and our destination, the Farmers' Museum, just across the street.

We're here for the wedding of my friends Carrie and Sherman. It's time to celebrate. It's time to dream of all that awaits them. And for me, the temptation to drift back into old memories, some of them fuzzy and some of them surprisingly vivid, is both inevitable and irresistible.

It was 45 years ago this summer that I first came here, with an anticipation and excitement that, for all its lack of sophistication, probably wasn't so different from what I'm feeling now, watching Carrie get married. I was all of 11 in 1968. Carrie was a decade from being born not far away in Middleburgh. Sherman, too, had yet to be born at the other end of the state, by Buffalo, come to think of it.

Going to Cooperstown and the Baseball Hall of Fame was both the first time I'd ever gone quite that far away and the first trip I ever took without my parents. A motel with a heated pool and color TVs in every room was a childhood luxury.

I was with my friend Pancho, Fran as he was known then, and his family. His father was a history professor, and summers were for excursions like this—to Cooperstown, Fort Ticonderoga, Hyde Park. I was seeing upstate New York two decades before I moved here and came to call it home.

Pancho's parents were still in their late 30s, younger than my own parents, but old nonetheless, it seemed, to a kid who was just beginning to fight off his own innocence. And here I am now, at 56, married but with no kids of our own, quite close in age to Carrie's mother, Cathy, wondering what it must be like to watch your offspring at their own weddings.

The grounds of the Farmers' Museum, so green and well attended, are a very new and fresh sight. What I remember of my one time here—I was lured by little more than baseball, after all—was the tractor where we could clamber about. Did tour guides use terms like *interactive playthings* then, I wonder?

I had no memory, certainly, of the Cornwallville Church, a small, starkly beautiful late 18th-century chapel that was built in the Greene County town of East Durham and was later the home of the Methodist Episcopal congregation not far away in Cornwallville. Here it is now, adjacent to the circa-1917 Main Barn at the Farmers' Museum. The Greek Revival elements bring your gaze first up to the balcony and then around the pews. There's not a trace of tourism in this plain but strikingly powerful place of worship.

How many weddings, I wonder, over how many generations, were performed here? How many lives were changed by even the briefest of ceremonies and the exchanges of the simplest vows?

For Carrie and Sherman, the wedding proceedings are reverent, moving, and very much to the point. I'm struck that my more casual friend Walter, a Catholic deacon now, is the officiant. I first knew him as the official spokesman for one of those public entities charged with maintaining ethics in a state government too often incapable of such a thing.

The reception takes place in the Main Barn's Louis C. Jones Center, a reception hall and gathering space where modern architecture has been incorporated into the fieldstone of the barn's façade. The original wooden beams soar above in the main foyer and atrium. It's a perfect atmosphere for a party that strikes me as offering upstate New York at its best, with an understated beauty and a distinct absence of pretense.

The lawns outside are an equally attractive setting for mingling and, of course, photos. As the evening light fades, the surrounding countryside seems even more majestic. It seems counterintuitive to so much as think of leaving a place that, tonight at least, isn't so out of bounds when it declares itself "America's most perfect village."

Cathy tells us about the Schoharie Valley farm she helps to operate, and how her house over in Middleburgh survived the latest of the unrelenting summer storms and floods. Carrie's father, John, is off to a relative's summer camp by Otsego Lake before he heads back to Florida. Carrie's brother, Chris, active in local politics in nearby Cherry Valley, talks about the damage that hydraulic fracturing for natural gas could do to the environment of upstate New York.

Darryl and I and Pete do head out of town, though. It seems right for this trip back to Cooperstown that we have baseball on the radio, a Red Sox game on the West Coast. Pete recalls how that sound reminds him of his own childhood journeys through the more distant reaches of New York.

Carrie and Sherman and seemingly everyone else are staying at inns maybe a mile away in Cooperstown. We're off to Sharon Springs, itself a thriving village to the north that attracted thousands of visitors a day until the construction of the Thruway 60 years ago turned it into something of a backwater.

The road back to Sharon Springs is an arduous one, as it is in so much of upstate New York. The great lure there these days is the American Hotel, with accommodations and a restaurant that are the rave of the high-priced set.

It's on the advice of the people at the American that we book much more reasonably priced rooms—about $150, thanks to some sort of deal—at a delightful bed-and-breakfast known as the New York House.

The place is huge enough that it's not hard at all to imagine it as the boardinghouse it was built as in 1885. Now it, too, is bouncing back, with its appeal to a clientele, we're told, that's more attracted to the regional arts scene than to the Hall of Fame.

The conversation at breakfast the next morning, not surprisingly, is all about the wedding, how much we enjoyed ourselves and, of course, how stunning Carrie looked.

We lingered for a time on the enormous front porch at the New York House, with its rocking chairs and lemonade fountain, chatting with the innkeepers, Kelly and Bruce. I had thoughts of going back into Cooperstown, to the souvenir shops and other monuments to baseball that enthralled me as an 11-year-old and perhaps to lunch at the Doubleday Café, a mainstay of more recent visits.

Instead, we were Albany-bound. Again, my mind was wandering while Darryl drove. Cooperstown and the area around it will always be intensely special for Carrie and Sherman, of course. But I already was thinking of the family that they might have, and how this part of upstate New York will be every bit as idyllic for another generation, and more after that.

Editors' note: Jim died four days after the publication of this story. Carrie Barown Jewett, the bride in this piece, read Carl Sandburg's poem "Chicago" at Jim's memorial service, September 14, 2013.

APPRECIATIONS

(Page 157)

Jim was never more relaxed than when he was at the outer end of Cape Cod, where he and Darryl spent part of their honeymoon in the summer of 2001. He had worked as the assistant to the shellfish warden in Scituate, Massachusetts, during a college summer, and the training that job instilled in him led him to later follow the tide charts during his Cape vacations almost as closely as he did the Red Sox scores. His contentment at being near the ocean shows in this undated photograph, taken in the early 2000s. Photograph by Darryl McGrath.

Jim McGrath's Albany

Fred LeBrun

Jim McGrath aptly described politics as "Albany's only major league sport." He did so love to watch the game, in all its complexities and entanglements, rivalries and alliances. At every level, from the state house on the hill down to the humblest South End ward. Such fertile ground for a political junkie. Being a transplanted Bostonian, small wonder he immediately felt comfortable, intrigued, by the dynamics of what made Albany tick and sought out every strand that gave him revelation. It was his gift to us that he had all that Irishness in his blood and brought fresh eyes to our old city and its open secrets.

Jim arrived here, as he mentions in a stellar piece in this collection, on a "warm October afternoon" and luckily found himself at a bar stool at the Lark Tavern. Lucky for us too. A first impression that was a portal to his heart. He was hooked. This was his kind of place, and over time a genuine affection developed and grew that permeated his writing. Editorial writing with affection for the frequent subject of political Albany, but also with a practiced eye for the warts, the shortcomings, the should be's, and the should have been's. His arrival in town was two years after the death of mayor Erastus Corning 2nd at, fittingly, a Boston hospital, a passing that was a major benchmark in Albany's long and complex political history.

Jim did experience firsthand the Mayor Tom Whalen era. Tom could be a difficult and irascible sort but in fairness left a considerable legacy as a reformer. We pick up the narrative of the Albany political story through Jim's editorial writing with the era that followed, that of Mayor Jerry Jennings. Jennings is a complicated character who started out as an outsider maverick with insider connections. He beat the political machine in a bruising battle and proved, for a few terms at least, to be a better than expected mayor with a great feel for street politics. But he could also be insular, and prone to arrogance and vindictiveness, as Jim records, as with Jerry's attempted outsized paybacks to rival Jack McEneny and his family. At the end of his time in office, Jerry Jennings was much like the insiders he displaced to begin with, although arguably he too moved the city forward.

By personal bent, Jim was a progressive Democrat, probably more liberal than the majority of his readers. Although you would not recognize that in his editorials. He could also be, in the conversational combat which he doted on, which we all loved, impetuous, intemperate, even outrageous in a tumble of forceful oratory that was his trademark. But that never showed in his writings. In print he was thoughtful, generous, sympathetic, never cynical, and his words were always laced with the wry wit he seemed to come by naturally. He took the time to get it right and never showed disrespect for his adopted city, or for others who loved it too but may not have entirely shared his views. He managed his passion with elegance, I suppose, even felt compelled to, "because this is Albany, and always someone is keeping score." Again, lucky us, that premier among them was Jim McGrath.

Fred LeBrun has been a reporter, editor, and metro columnist for the Albany *Times Union* since 1967.

Jim McGrath

A Newspaperman

Robert Whitcomb

I was born a decade before Jim McGrath but he always seemed a member of my generation of the dwindling group we usually called "newspapermen" (not "journalists"). And that's not just because of his, shall we say, relaxed sartorial standards and love of certain watering holes as venues for creative conversation and fact-finding.

He was from Boston (where his father was a newspaper printer!), and his dedication to making a news story, a column, or an editorial as good as it could be in the face of unforgiving deadlines, along with his conviviality and sense of humor, reminded me of what I first experienced during my time as a Boston newspaperman for two now-long-dead newspapers—the *Record American* and *Herald-Traveller*. We had a lot of joy despite the daily work pressures in those days, albeit often doing things not recommended by the American Medical Association. (I suppose there will soon be very few city newspapers—which is good news for crooks of all kinds but particularly for political crooks, whom Jim was expert at identifying, in Albany and elsewhere.)

To some extent, Jim remained a Boston Irishman his whole life, in his unusual mix of tough, skeptical observer and romantic, about his beloved Red Sox, and some other things. And I'd guess that his rigorous education at the famous Boston Latin School helped make him the disciplined writer and editor he became.

Jim was also an old-fashioned newspaperman in that he worked for a bunch of papers before he settled down at the *Times Union*. "Itinerant newspaperman" used to be a common creature.

We had mutual friends, but I didn't get to know him until he started writing occasional columns for the *Providence Journal*, where I was editorial page editor for a couple of decades.

As I started following his career, I found he could do it all—write with elegance and controlled passion, edit and rewrite with great precision, lay out pages, and do a bunch of other stuff needed to put out newspapers every day. But then, he spent his entire working career in the business, enjoying its last 20 years of prosperity before the Internet and ever-more myopic newspaper chain ownership started to destroy it.

His columns for me (and everyone) ranged over a very wide range of subjects—he could comment on almost any topic with clarity, concision, and lasting persuasiveness—aided by his immense reading and astounding recall. But politics and government (and the need for constant vigilance thereof), the environment, sports, and history were major areas. While he could joke around with the sort of cynicism often associated with veteran journalists who had seen too much bad behavior, his drive for finding the truth, explaining it to citizens, and laying out to them the best ways to respond to it never wavered. Think of how much healthier our civic life would be if we had many more people like Jim McGrath.

Jim could be voluble and shout an argument, but he was a softie—an affectionate man, devoted of course to Darryl and his wider family but also to an extraordinarily wide range of friends of all walks of life. I do like to think, however, that he had a particular affection for other journalists, and especially those like us who had had ringside seats to good and bad times over the decades and had a few beers while watching the show.

Robert Whitcomb is a Providence-based editor and writer, former editor at the *International Herald Tribune*, and the *Wall Street Journal,* and former editorial-page editor of the *Providence Journal*. He published many of Jim's essays in the *Providence Journal*'s editorial pages.

APPENDIX

Jim enjoying a visit in October 2004 to the Oak Street Beach along Lake Michigan, just off Michigan Avenue in downtown Chicago. The Oak Street Beach was a favorite place for Jim and Darryl during their courtship and honeymoon in Chicago, and Darryl later scattered a portion of Jim's ashes into the lake from the beach. Photograph by Darryl McGrath.

Meet My Not-So-Silent Partner

DAN LYNCH

Times Union column, June 11, 1996

McGrath was on the phone.

"Bad news," he was saying. "You're long again." I said something highly inelegant in response.

"I can fix it, though," he assured me.

Then McGrath led me through it. We could take out this word here, that phrase there. We could combine these two paragraphs and pick up a line. And by the way, did I really want to say this that way? Wouldn't it be better to say it this way?

And, as usual, it would be.

I've been writing this column for about a year now—roughly 200 of them in the paper since last June. Four times a week, I try to tell you a little something you might not know, maybe offer you some insight into something you hadn't thought of. That's what a columnist does—a little news, a little snappy patter, a little razzle-dazzle.

Now, let me tell you what Jim McGrath does. Most days, he saves my butt. Outside the *Times Union* newsroom nobody knows that, so I thought I'd mention it to you.

McGrath is a tall, bearded guy about 40 who looks like Grizzly Adams's younger brother. Actually, he's the younger brother of Chip McGrath, the editor of the *New York Times Book Review*—in which, incidentally, none of my books have been reviewed. Just thought I'd mention that stirring injustice in case I ever write another one.

McGrath is a copy editor, one of the interior linemen of daily journalism. These people edit the stories and columns in the newspaper, decide how the photographs will be displayed, write the headlines and photo captions, and put the whole package together. They labor late into the night, working under intense deadline pressure on complex computers, literally sweating at times even though they move hardly an inch when an edition is due. It's the sort of perspiration you see in the television shows about hospitals—the drenching sweat of intense, surgical concentration.

When I started this thing, I was asked who I wanted as an editor. McGrath's name naturally came to mind. He's a pro—in his own right, as good a writer as you'll find in this business, and an unreconstructed newspaper junkie, like I am.

It's in his blood. McGrath came out of Boston, the son of a newspaper printer. He managed to get into some ritzy college and actually graduated. Then he went to work for operations like the Hollywood, Florida, *Sun-Tattler*, a newspaper with absolutely the best name in the industry. Eventually, he came to work for our now-defunct *Knickerbocker News*. When the *Knick* died, he was absorbed by the *Times Union*—and grudgingly, too.

McGrath is mouthy. I knew that because he used to work for me. I knew, too, that if he'd mouth off to the managing editor, I could trust him to give me his best judgment when he thought something in the column could be better said.

He's done that. Every night when I file this thing, I check later by phone with McGrath, who's been awake only a few hours because copy desk work forces you into vampire sleeping habits. I tend to write long. McGrath always imposes economy on my thoughts without savaging my (ahem) elegant and poetic style.

So, if you see a column you like—one that blinds you with its brilliance and the grace of its language—you can thank me. If you see one that doesn't quite work, blame McGrath. That's what I always do.

Times Union Editorial Writer Appointed

Times Union, November 7, 1996

James M. McGrath has been named chief editorial writer of the *Times Union* by editor Harry M. Rosenfeld.

Mr. McGrath replaces Dan Davidson, who is resigning to pursue other interests.

The appointment is effective November 18. Mr. McGrath will report to Howard Healy, the editorial page editor.

Jim McGrath, 39, a native of Boston, joined the *Knickerbocker News* as a news editor in 1985 and became a member of the *Times Union* staff upon the merger of the two newspapers in 1988.

In addition to various editing assignments, Mr. McGrath has been an occasional contributor to the editorial and op-ed pages.

He was educated at Lake Forest College in Illinois and was awarded a graduate degree in journalism from Northwestern University.

Earlier newspaper experience includes the *News-Sun* in Waukegan, Illinois, the *Hartford Courant*, and the *Sun-Tattler* in Hollywood, Florida.

Guild Mourns the Loss of Jim McGrath

Albany Newspaper Guild website, September 5, 2013

The Guild deeply mourns the loss of our dear colleague Jim McGrath. The news-paper's chief editorial writer, Jim was a longtime supporter of the Guild, even when he was no longer a member, always stopping to offer words of encouragement. We send our condolences to his wife Darryl and his family.

McGrath's Keen Eye, Passion Recalled

Times Union's Chief Editorial Writer, 56, Died While Vacationing

Steve Barnes

Times Union, September 6, 2013

Jim McGrath, a lifelong journalist who had newspaper ink in his blood but who would have grimaced at the cliché, died suddenly Wednesday night of a heart attack while vacationing on Cape Cod. Under treatment for a serious cardiac condition for the past two years, he was 56 and had been the chief editorial writer of the *Times Union* since 1996.

Known equally for his keen political eye, for his love of the Red Sox of his native Boston, and for the long-billed Hemingway-style cap that he invariably wore when not at work, McGrath was an exceptional figure on a contemporary editorial board.

In a room of groomed, business-attired journalists interviewing similarly dressed politicians or other leaders seeking blessing or forgiveness from the *Times Union's* editorial page, McGrath stood out. His beard bristled, his eyes squinted behind unstylish glasses, his speech stutter-started when making vigorous points, and his hair fringed down in the back from a bald dome. One colleague said Thursday he looked like an off-kilter Muppet; another described him as a Dr. Seuss character or a combination of absent-minded professor, walrus, and Einstein.

Regardless, McGrath's head encased a brain acute with ideas and perspectives. His work won many journalism awards, including during each of the past nine years. His most recent two, announced last week by the New York State Associated Press Association, were second- and third-place awards, respectively, for editorials on dysfunction in the Ravena-Coeymans-Selkirk school district and on the reaction of New York state politicians to Governor Andrew Cuomo's gun-control legislation.

"He was . . . the conscience of this community," said Phil Calderone, Albany's deputy mayor and friend of McGrath's for 17 years. The pair were largely anonymous in a similar way: McGrath the voice behind most of the newspaper's unsigned editorials about the city of Albany, Calderone the top behind-the-scenes operator at City Hall. The two had lunch regularly and spoke more often, usually about Albany issues. "You could feel the passion he had for the city," Calderone said. "An editorial wouldn't have his name on it, but you could tell when it was Jim's and what he was feeling."

Mayor Jerry Jennings said, "What I always appreciated was how he made sure he had the complete story before he wrote something. He was always open to discussion—and to disagreement, if necessary—and that's what made it such a pleasure to talk to him." Jennings ordered the flags at City Hall lowered to half-staff Thursday afternoon in McGrath's honor.

McGrath was also, when he penned the occasional personal column, a word-smith of casual, gentle eloquence. Writing in the *Times Union* on August 25 about a visit to Cooperstown for the wedding of friends, he connected the trip with the first one he'd made to see the home of the Baseball Hall of Fame 45 years before, as a boy of 11: "It's time to celebrate. It's time to dream of all that awaits them. And for me, the temptation to drift back into old memories, some of them fuzzy and some of them surprisingly vivid, is both inevitable and irresistible."

"Few people truly achieve the status of legends in their lifetimes, but Jim McGrath was already that in our newsroom," *Times Union* editor Rex Smith said. "Now we're left to cherish the memory of not only his professional skill, but also of his personal brilliance, passion, and kindness."

Born June 4, 1957, in Boston's Brighton neighborhood as one of four children in an Irish Catholic family, McGrath was the son of a newspaper printer and a homemaker. Educated at Boston Latin School and Lake Forest College and Northwestern University, the latter two north of Chicago, McGrath began his career at the *News-Sun* in Waukegan, Illinois.

He started as a copy editor at the *Times Union*'s former sister paper, the *Knickerbocker News*, in 1985. When that paper closed in 1988, McGrath moved up through the copyediting ranks at the *Times Union* until he was the night copy desk chief, engaging readers with arresting headlines and preventing writers from seeing their mistakes make it into print.

Former *Times Union* managing editor and columnist Dan Lynch, who chose McGrath to edit his four-times-a-week column in the late 1990s, put it this way in a column: "Now, let me tell you what Jim McGrath does. Most days, he saves my butt." After praising the deftness of McGrath's editing, Lynch added, "in his own right, [he's] as good a writer as you'll find in this business."

As an editorialist, McGrath took special interest in writing about Albany, national politics, and environmental issues, said Jay Jochnowitz, the *Times Union*'s editorial page editor. McGrath devoured the *Times Union* and the *New York Times* daily, and he was famed in-house for the speed of his reading, sometimes responding with thoughts and suggested changes within minutes of Jochnowitz having finished a piece.

"I always enjoyed the opportunity to debate the issues with Jim in the *Times Union* editorial board meetings," said US Representative Chris Gibson, R-Kinderhook. "He and his writing will be missed."

McGrath was equally quick in his assessments of the inner workings of the newspaper office, limning developments and personnel moves as they occurred—or even before. When colleagues wanted to know what was really happening at work, they asked him. And he could be voluble to the point of explosiveness. About a dozen years ago, a new senior manager went to investigate a shouted argument in McGrath's office and returned with a stricken expression. She said, "Jim just asked me, 'What the (expletive) is your problem?' I don't know whether he was joking or not."

McGrath loved journalism to the exclusion of most everything except his wife, Darryl, his friends, and sports. For many years he drove battered cars, wore khakis at work and jeans or shorts elsewhere, often with T-shirts and, not unusually, a glossy Red Sox jacket. The jacket was so distinctive that it was part of the costume one of McGrath's younger bar friends, Matt Walczak, wore when he dressed as McGrath for Halloween a few years ago, complete with white beard and the same Hemingway cap from the J. Peterman catalog.

McGrath was a boisterous friend to his closest companions, greeting them with a "Huh-ho!" chortle and a big arm swing into a handshake or backslap. In earlier years in Albany he seemed more reserved with new acquaintances, and so Tess Collins, who ran a succession of watering holes McGrath frequented, made a point to introduce him to as many people as she could, Walczak among them. "The younger people—they just loved him, and he really opened up as he got older," Collins said Thursday between bouts of tears. She described her staff at McGeary's, who had come to love McGrath during their years at the former Tess' Lark Tavern and later downtown at McGeary's, as devastated by the news of his death.

"Jim was the kind of guy you could meet randomly at a bar on Lark Street, and one beer would turn into seven as he'd discuss politics, journalism, and baseball," said Rob Gavin, who covers courts for the *Times Union*. He said, "For a guy with a world of esoteric knowledge about many areas, he never put on airs."

"He wore his heart on his sleeve," said Calderone. "Whether he was feeling joy or pain about a topic, that would come through in the editorials."

McGrath's joy would have been effusive late Wednesday—or perhaps his spirit had already moved from Wellfleet, where he and his wife had been vacationing on Cape Cod, to a celebratory Fenway Park in Boston. His beloved Red Sox romped all over the Detroit Tigers, taking home a 20-4 win that included a grand slam and seven more home runs, tying a team record.

McGrath is survived by his wife, Darryl, of Albany; two brothers, Charles "Chip" McGrath of New Jersey and Tom McGrath of Milton, Massachusetts; a sister, Mary McGrath, also of Milton; six nieces and nephews; a great-niece and three great-nephews.

A memorial service will be held at 1 p.m. Saturday, September 14, at Trinity United Methodist Church, 235 Lark Street, Albany.

McGrath, who regained sight in one eye after receiving a cornea transplant, wanted his organs to be donated, his wife said. Financial contributions may be made in his name to Lake Forest College, 555 N. Sheridan Road, Lake Forest, Illinois, 60045.

James M. McGrath, 1957–2013

Times Union EDITORIAL BOARD

Times Union, editorial pages, September 8, 2013

This page will look mostly the way it always does next week, and the weeks after that. But in one way, it will never be the same.

We lost one of our own on Wednesday. Jim McGrath, the *Times Union*'s chief editorial writer since 1996, died of a heart attack while vacationing with his wife on Cape Cod.

Regular readers of this page no doubt have noticed that there are different voices in our editorials from day to day. Many have had a complex, rather literary quality to them. That was Jim's irrepressible voice and eloquent style coming through, no matter what the issue, whether it was on Albany, the city he loved, or the environment, one of his great interests, or any of the countless injustices, political foibles, and complex issues he tackled over the years.

Monday morning would have brought Jim back from vacation, no doubt dressed, as always, for casual Friday, fortified with a tall coffee and ready to engage with the rest of the editorial board with his booming voice and incisive views. It would have had him back at his keyboard, whispering out loud as he composed to make sure not just that the words were right, but that they sounded right. We brace for the silence.

Readers of this page also probably notice that we broke a rule today. Our tradition in editorials is to address people as "Mr." or "Ms." Pardon us for dispensing with formalities this once, but Jim would have scoffed at "Mr. McGrath." So, Jim it is.

So long, Jim. And forgive us for being so brief, but we have lost our voice.

Obituary

WRITTEN BY DARRYL MCGRATH

Times Union, September 12, 2013

Albany—Jim McGrath, 56, the longtime chief editorial writer for the Albany *Times Union*, died September 4, 2013, at Cape Cod Hospital in Hyannis, Massachusetts. He had been diagnosed in 2011 with a serious cardiac condition and died of a heart attack while helping his wife, Darryl, get to the hospital for treatment of a severe allergic reaction. His wife was treated and released.

He was an organ donor, a decision he made after being the recipient of a donated cornea a decade earlier.

He was born June 4, 1957, in Brighton, Massachusetts, to Charles McGrath, a newspaper printer, and Catherine McGrail McGrath, a homemaker. He graduated from Boston Latin School and Lake Forest College in Lake Forest, Illinois, where he graduated with honors with a dual degree in sociology and anthropology. An accomplished soccer player, he helped the Lake Forest varsity men's soccer team win the Midwest Conference championship in 1975 and 1976. He was editor of the college newspaper, the *Stentor*, and also served on the college's judicial board.

He earned a master's degree at Northwestern University's Medill School of Journalism in Chicago, Illinois, in 1982, and started his professional newspaper career at the *News-Sun* in Waukegan, Illinois. He subsequently worked at newspapers in Massachusetts, Florida, and Connecticut, including the *Hartford Courant*, as a reporter, editor, and editorial page columnist before joining the *Knickerbocker News* in Albany as a news editor in 1985. When that newspaper closed in 1988, he joined the *Times Union* as a copy editor and eventually was named copy desk chief. He was a frequent guest writer of opinion pieces and editorials for the *Times Union* before becoming the paper's chief editorial writer in 1996. He specialized in politics, economics, social issues, the environment, and sports. In the past decade, he had written numerous guest opinion pieces for *Newsday* and the *Providence Journal*. He received numerous state and national awards for his editorials. He was named the Hearst Editorial Writer of the Year several times and also received numerous first- and second-place awards by the New York State Associated Press Association and two first-place awards by the New York News Publishers Association.

He was a Knight Center Fellow at the University of Maryland in 1997, and was a corecipient, along with other *Times Union* staff, of the Investigative Reporters and Editors' 2007 Freedom of Information Medal for a series about spending by state lawmakers. He was also corecipient with the other editorial board members of

Common Cause's 2002 "I Love an Ethical New York" award for a series of editorials on campaign finance reform and Freedom of Information compliance by state lawmakers.

He was a voracious reader, an enthusiastic baseball fan, and an avid bicyclist, canoeist, and camper.

He had been predeceased by his parents while in college. In addition to his wife, he is survived by his brothers, Charles McGrath of Allendale, New Jersey, and Thomas McGrath, of Milton, Massachusetts; a sister, Mary McGrath, also of Milton; six nieces and nephews; one great-niece and three great-nephews.

A memorial service will be held 1 p.m. Saturday (September 14) at Trinity United Methodist Church, 235 Lark Street, Albany. Burial will be private. Because of Darryl McGrath's severe allergies, the family emphatically asks that flowers not be sent to the home or the church.

Memorial contributions can be made to the student newspaper at Lake Forest College, *The Stentor*, c/o Lake Forest College, 555 N. Sheridan Road, Lake Forest, Illinois 60045.

Eulogy

DARRYL McGRATH

Trinity United Methodist Church, Lark Street, Albany, September 14, 2013

There are some people I would first like to acknowledge and welcome. Mayor Jennings; Deputy Mayor Calderone; members of the Albany Common Council; and the honored representatives of our state, county, and city governments. From the *Times Union*: Publisher George Hearst; editor Rex Smith and his wife Marion; current and emeritus members of the *Times Union* editorial board. My sisters and brothers from the Albany Newspaper Guild are here in support of their "Exempt Brother." Now you know who was writing all those blog posts on the Guild website. I would also like to welcome my McGrath family members, who have all been so wonderful these past 10 days, even through their own grief, as well as so many of Jim's friends and colleagues. My own family could not be here today, as my mother is 93 years old and has been devastated by Jim's death, and my family members are right where they should be, comforting my mother at her home in Connecticut.

Thank you all for being here and honoring Jim with your presence, your love, your laughter, and, today, your tears. Jim would have looked out at this wonderful and varied assemblage and he would not only have thought that this was exactly what he deserved—he would have also told us all that.

And then he would have told me to go get a pen, so that he could tighten up this lede.

A little more than 12 years ago, many of you watched in a rose garden in Buffalo as Jim promised to always be my best friend, to honor me, and to ennoble me.

Today, I stand before you in Jim's beloved adopted city as I face the impossible task of summing up, in the same brief amount of time, the astonishing life of my brilliant, irreverent, irrepressible, outrageous, and all-around amazing husband, Jim McGrath. Jim would have told me to do it up nice. I will do it up in a way that I hope would make him proud, because he and I talked about this day. We had an early warning two springs ago that this might be coming down the road at us, and Jim made some very specific requests that I have tried to capture here.

You have heard today from people who knew Jim far longer than I did, and in very different ways. I was always very aware that I was a tagline in Jim's life, the person who signed on for the last 15 years but who had nothing of the history that so many others had shared with him. So I will share with you the qualities that made me decide to sign on, and that made those 15 years pure magic.

First: Jim identified with people who needed both forgiveness and a break. He championed marriage equality so that everyone in New York could live in a legally recognized relationship with the person they love. He championed our friend John O'Hara, who needed a powerful voice when a political machine tried to silence John's activism by wrongfully convicting him of illegal voting. And John, if the governor had honored us with his presence today, I would have asked him to pardon you, and he probably would have done it for me today.

But Jim's concern and compassion for the underdog are best illustrated in a story that never made it into the *Times Union*. This is the story of a former student of mine whom I will call "Mr. Stein," and who hailed from a blue-collar family on Staten Island. This is, by the way, the one anecdote that Jim asked me to include in his memorial service.

I had Mr. Stein in a fall semester class in 2006, the same year that the Mets were in a playoff with the St. Louis Cardinals for the National League pennant. Mr. Stein came to see me in my campus office, in full Mets regalia—the cap, the baseball jersey—and asked if he could miss an upcoming class, because his mother had procured tickets to the game for him. I told him, "Mr. Stein, you can indeed miss class as an excused absence, because you came and asked me, and also because you're never going to see the Mets do this again."

So, come the end of the semester, and Mr. Stein is very likely to get a C for his course grade, and it was not because he did not try. Maybe a C-plus if I stretched it. So I put the case to Jim. And, because my program director from the university is here, Nancy, I promise, I did this without breaching student confidentiality. I explained the student's circumstances to Jim, how this student was the first kid in his family to go to college, how he was trying so hard, and how he had almost certainly grown up in a home where his parents loved him but no one did a lot of reading or writing.

And Jim was able to overcome the fact that Mr. Stein was rooting for the Mets instead of Boston, and he said, "Give him a B-minus. Because if you give this kid a C, you're going to kill his confidence. And if he's trying as hard as you say, and he's a good kid, chances are that you could make a very legitimate case for the B-minus. This way, he can go home at Christmas and tell all his friends who are working at the Staten Island recycling center that he's doing B-level work at the state university."

So I did as Jim suggested. And Mr. Stein, if you ever hear this story, you have Jim to thank for that particular grade, and I do know that you graduated four years later. I hope you are doing well.

Second: Jim had great compassion for the people the rest of us never notice—the homeless, the abused, the unwashed, and the ignored. He wrote an op-ed piece in 2001 about a man named Phil Caiozzo, who died after going into alcohol withdrawal in a county jail following his arrest on a minor public nuisance charge. I thought this was one of the most eloquent and compelling pieces Jim ever wrote, and whenever he was going through his body of work to decide what to submit for a fellowship application, I would urge him to include this piece. It is too long to read in its entirety, but I did want to include an excerpt, because it speaks to Jim's ability to see people with, for lack of a better term, tenderness.

The piece was entitled: "A Lesson Taught Too Late."

> The ruined life of Phil Caiozzo, all those years on the streets and in homeless shelters, ought to have this legacy. No one should die the way he did.
>
> Caiozzo was 48 when he died last week, a few hours after suffering from convulsions first experienced in a cell at the Albany County Jail. . . .
>
> Five years ago, Caiozzo was hospitalized following the severe withdrawal that came after one of his arrests. So it also was known, then, what happens so easily to people in his stage of the brutal disease of alcoholism. . . .
>
> These people will cease drinking in custody, of course—but with often traumatic results. The convulsions Caiozzo suffered are part of a hard-core alcoholic's all-too-frequent pain. That's why there are beds in emergency detoxification wards. The procedure more commonly known as drying out requires a level of medical supervision considerably more sophisticated than a jail provides. . . .
>
> This is what society wanted from Caiozzo, and still wants from the dozens of other alcoholics on the streets of Albany. To stop drinking, and to behave. It's not easy, not remotely easy. Not for those whose lives have hit the bottom, and not for the fortunate majority living in their midst, getting hit up for spare change and trying to step over them. . . .
>
> Of Caiozzo, it might be said that he died at the wrong time, in the wrong place. . . .
>
> Let his painful and shortened life amount to this much—a lasting reminder of the depths of alcoholism, how to confront that and how not to.

Finally: Jim made me feel completely, unconditionally loved in a way that very few people experience. He truly never got angry with me, he compromised very well, and he had great confidence in me. Jim's philosophy about life in general and marriage in particular could be summed up in four expressions—we called them "Jimisms"—which I heard every week of our married life, and which I have found myself saying often in this first full week of my new life alone. Those expressions were: "Follow your instincts; you always make the right decision." "No fuss, no muss." I actually had to look up the word "muss" in *Webster's*. It's a real word; it means to rearrange something. Then there was, "We have it good," and finally,

"Play poker with Milwaukee." That last was Jim's advice to me when I thought I might have competing job offers between Buffalo and Milwaukee, and it became our metaphor for skillful bargaining.

During our courtship, the paper in Austin, Texas, was very interested in luring Jim out there for an editorial writer's position. He asked me if I would go to Texas with him if the job came through, and I said "Yes" without any hesitation. Then, it turned out that the paper in Austin was interested in *both* of us. We had a date for an interview in Texas, we were looking at airline reservations, I bought an outfit . . . those of you who are here from the newspaper business know where this story is going. A few weeks after Jim asked me if I would move with him, the Austin paper had what we newspaper people call a "Saturday night massacre" in its newsroom, and the following Monday morning, all of the editors at the paper either had a different job from the one they had left Friday night or no job at all. And in that massive reshuffling of the newsroom, the offer from Austin vaporized. But my willingness to drop everything and go with this man stunned me.

That episode came back to me as we planned our marriage ceremony. Jim was raised a Roman Catholic, and although he had long ago left behind the active observance of his faith, he never entirely gave up on his Catholic beliefs. So my husband's Catholicism popped up in surprising ways. Jim had no problem with being married in a Protestant marriage ceremony, and in fact when I asked him if he would prefer a Catholic nuptial Mass, he said, "You can have one if you want it, but I won't be there." He was all the more pleasantly intrigued by the idea of a Protestant wedding when he learned that the Protestant ceremony does not include holy communion, which Jim called "the magic show." We got around his surprising pre–Vatican II objection to being married *inside* the physical structure of another denomination's house of worship by getting married outdoors.

But then we hit a stumbling block. I guess I still had that almost-move to Austin on my mind, and I wanted to have our minister, the wonderful Reverend Darius Pridgen, quote a passage from the Old Testament book of Ruth that I felt captured the spirit of the day. Jim thought this passage was way too heavy, and he also wanted to keep this short and sweet and get to the party. So in our last meeting with our minister, on the day before our wedding, we put this dilemma to Pastor Pridgen. I told him what passage I wanted, and I told him of Jim's objections. Darius turned to me and said, "Does this scripture passage reflect how you really feel?" And I said, "It expresses how I feel, but if Jim is not comfortable with it, I can skip it." An early lesson in marital compromise.

But because I have never forgotten my initial feeling that this passage captured the essence of binding my life to Jim's life, as well as my willingness to take a leap and move to Texas, I will recite it here. And Jim was right—it didn't belong in our wedding ceremony, but I could never have predicted that I would say it for him in another context, quite so soon. It works in both situations, because it speaks to the irrational blind faith that you need not just to get married, but to make that marriage last. It reads:

Entreat me not to leave thee, nor to return from following thee. Where you go, I will go. Where you dwell, I will dwell. Your people will be my people, your God will be my God, and where you die, there so shall I be buried. And may the Lord deal with me, be it ever so severely, if anything but death ever separates you and me.

Our last day was a day of gorgeous time on the beach and a lingering stroll down Commercial Street in Provincetown; of seeing my husband, who had a silly side, making faces at me through the window of a bookstore as I paid for my purchase; of eating a shared double scoop of sorbet at our favorite ice cream stand, and me watching in dismay as Jim ate all of the chocolate sprinkles off the top in two big bites—I am so glad I didn't say anything, and, no joke, a sunset over the Wellfleet Harbor that was surreal in its beauty.

Then, at twilight, we shared one very long hug standing by our car, which for some reason I remember very vividly. Perhaps because I found myself listening to Jim's heartbeat, which I always did when I thought he would not notice—it sounded steady and strong—and perhaps because we hugged just after we left that waterfront restaurant and just before we drove to an ocean beach for a nighttime stroll, about three minutes before everything changed.

We place a great value in this culture on identifying the first, the last, the best, the most. Journalists quickly learn that you never call anything the first or the last, because the minute that you do, the other 50 firsts and lasts come out of the woodwork and start yelling at you. But I do want to tell you Jim's last words to me, which I value all the more because we did not have a chance to say good-bye and we did not have a final chance to tell each other, "I love you."

Instead, we had a hasty parting as the paramedics buckled me onto a gurney and got ready to load me into the ambulance. Jim could not bend down and kiss me or hug me because he could not get that close to me at that moment, and so instead, he grabbed my shoulders from behind. And I remember noticing the strength of his grip. He said to me, "You're going to be OK." And then he said it again: *"You're going to be OK."*

So I would now say in turn to my beloved husband, "Sweetheart, you too are going to be OK. Where you are right now, you're going to have no more pills, no more heart attacks, no more feeling afraid, no more wracking pain from the side effects of the medications, no more fatigue, no more endless doctor's appointments, and no more anxiety. You are going to be OK forever, and I promise you: So will I."

Remembering Albany's Voice of Reason

LAUREN MINEAU

Albany Student Press, State University of New York, Albany,
October 4, 2013

Every Tuesday and Thursday morning this summer, I was greeted by one of the most brilliant minds in the Capital Region and maybe all of journalism. Jim McGrath, chief editorial writer for the Albany *Times Union*, was passionate, boisterous, but most of all, the voice of the Albany's largest newspaper.

When I heard about Jim's passing, I couldn't find words. I can almost always find words, and Jim is one of the reasons why.

A conversation with Jim was never easy, but it was always worth it. You'd always take away something. I'm naturally soft-spoken and between his hearing aids and his brilliant mind buzzing with ideas and perspective, I understand how my words could get lost.

Each morning he'd come into the office I was fortunate enough to share with him, armed with newspapers, a large coffee, and always sported a Hemingway-style cap. On this year's hot July days, his glasses would be foggy from outside as he'd squint at the day's headlines.

His passion for journalism and Albany was always evident. He was fair and never went with a story until he had all the sides and time to weigh them equally. His passion was so strong, he'd often be in his "groove" and I wouldn't hear from him for hours as he wrote.

Jim wrote about UAlbany a few times during my internship, and he'd always ask me what I thought of what he had written or if his facts were correct. I was honored. On my last day, he wished me luck at the *ASP* and left me with a "Take care, Lauren, I'll see you soon."

He was genuine and always eager to teach me something new. He'd always show me the next day's page layout and ask me what I thought. I'm not sure if it was his genuine kindness or his actual need for another person's thoughts. I'll never know, but I'm going to say it's a little of both.

His contributions in the morning meetings were always spot-on. I was amazed how quickly he could form an educated and nonbiased perspective on an issue that was newly presented to him. But that was Jim.

Jim loved to discuss his travels and his experiences. Although at 21, I didn't have much to add to the conversation, but he'd always tell me I had to travel in my lifetime. He was passionate about cities and the way they were structured.

He often spoke highly of Chicago and, of course, Boston, home to his beloved Red Sox.

Jim was the go-to guy for answers around the office. Throughout the day, newsroom colleagues would stop in with questions and he would always give them an answer. Many would leave disgruntled because it wasn't what they wanted to hear, but they knew he was right.

Sometimes I felt I could recite the next day's editorial verbatim after hearing Jim ponder the words out loud as he laced them together. Though the *Times Union*'s editorials are unsigned, one could always tell if Jim had written them; very few write the way Jim did. Jim McGrath was one of a kind, and, if he edited this piece, he'd immediately delete that cliché. His unique personality and candor made him impossible to forget; I never will, and I suspect the city of Albany won't either.

As I write this, the Boston Red Sox have taken the lead in Friday's game versus the New York Yankees. As a die-hard Yanks fan, normally I would scoff at the thought of rooting for the Sox. However, tonight is different. Tonight, I smile as those bearded Bostonians round the bases, for you, Jim.

I'll miss you, Jim. More importantly, Albany will miss you. But we will never forget you. Rest easy, my friend.

Jim McGrath, chief editorial writer for the Albany *Times Union*, died Wednesday, September 4, while vacationing in Cape Cod with his wife, Darryl McGrath, who is a University at Albany journalism professor.

Editors' note: Lauren Mineau is the former editor-in-chief of the Albany Student Press, the campus newspaper of the State University of New York, Albany, and she was also Jim's last summer intern, through the UAlbany journalism program, in 2013, shortly before Jim's death.

Empowered to Do the Right Thing

Darryl McGrath

Times Union opinion piece, December 7, 2013

"Sweetheart, don't go any further down this road."

I tried to sound calm as I spoke to my husband, Jim, against the background of a Red Sox game on our car radio.

It was September 4, during our vacation on the remote end of Cape Cod. Barely 10 minutes earlier, we had finished dinner along the harbor. Then, as an astonishing sunset faded, we drove down a twisting, narrow beach road for a nighttime walk on the sand.

A minute earlier, I had felt congestion in my throat. I recognized the onset of an allergic reaction, as I had a history of such reactions to unidentifiable substances in foods. I carried an EpiPen, but I usually could treat myself with over-the-counter medication. Not this time, as a choking flood of secretions suddenly overwhelmed my airway. I remember thinking, "This is going way too fast," as I used my EpiPen. My symptoms only worsened.

At all costs, I did not want Jim to see my panic. He had suffered a major heart attack in 2011 and soon after was diagnosed with a serious heart condition. He responded well to drug treatments, and his recent checkups had been excellent, but I did not want to stress him.

Jim, however, knew how serious this was. He turned the car and raced back to the main road, even though we had no idea where to find help. I could still speak, and I told Jim to drive to a police station several miles away. Jim instead thought we should try a much closer building that looked like a fire station. We did not know if anyone was there, but we had to act fast: I was laboring to draw each breath.

A medical crew was on duty. Jim reached for me as I went into the ambulance. "You're going to be OK!" he said. A medic told Jim, "Follow us in your car!" as the ambulance headed 40 miles to Cape Cod Hospital.

Jim almost made it. Minutes from the hospital, he turned off the road, unnoticed, as the heart attack hit him. He ended up in the same emergency department where I frantically waited, convinced that he must have been pulled over for speeding. Our vacation that had started so magically ended with my screams of anguish as a nurse told me what had happened.

Friends have since asked me, how then, just minutes later, did I agree to organ donation?

First, the decision brought full circle another family's powerful choice of years earlier. Shortly before Jim and I married, he learned that he had a cornea disease, and in 2002, he had a transplant that restored sight in one eye. (The other eye stabilized.) The donor was a 27-year-old man. Jim, an editorial writer at the *Times Union*, talked up organ donation with his colleagues. Now, I had a chance to repay that gift, because Jim was approved as a bone and skin donor.

Second, the philosophy behind donation was in keeping with Jim's approach to life. My husband was the least materialistic person I had ever known, a brilliant, complex man of simple tastes and passionate convictions who could have put everything he valued except me into the backpack he carried to work. The idea that Jim could be a donor seemed empowering, and a triumph over the heart condition that killed him.

And finally, I had to leave the hospital that night with something more than the realization that my husband was dead. I needed to feel that this tragedy was not an ending for Jim and me, but a stunning change that would either break me or send me in some unknown but ultimately good direction. As a reporter, I had covered many horrific incidents, including the 1988 terrorist bombing of Pan Am Flight 103, and I was always astonished by the strength of the human spirit. I would leave an interview with a victim's family and think, How have these people survived? Now, I faced that question on my own.

Only a few months later, I don't have an answer, and I don't think I ever will. I do know that my decision to let Jim be a donor was the only light I could see in an otherwise terrible and dark time. At Jim's memorial service, I asked my minister to read the passage from Deuteronomy that includes the beloved lines "I set before you life and death, blessing and curse; therefore choose life . . ." Jim always told me to follow my instincts, because he always thought I made the right decision. So I chose what I hoped would be a continuation of life over death, and I believe that Jim would indeed have told me that I once again got it right.

Acknowledgments

We owe our first and greatest gratitude to Jim McGrath, who left such a distinctive mark on the *Times Union*'s writing and editorial positions. Jim also left several folders of neatly clipped and dated copies of what he apparently considered his best work and most important topics in his desk in the *Times Union*'s newsroom. These were discovered after his death, and their contents formed the basis of this book.

Jim also did something that is all too rare in today's world of digitalized journalism: He regularly got out, often on his own time, to see the places and talk to the people who populated his editorials. That's the reason, for example, that his description of the hometown of a soldier killed in Afghanistan makes readers feel like they too had traveled to that peaceful cemetery in the Berkshires, and why his portraits of Albany's neighborhoods are so vivid.

Thanks to Rex Smith, the *Times Union*'s editor, and to Mike Spain, the paper's associate editor, for their technical help with access to the paper's archives and for the readily granted permission to use copyrighted materials. The *Times Union* provided a forum that matched Jim's passions on so many topics, and on the comparatively rare occasions when Jim disagreed with the editorial board's position, well, he made sure everyone knew it. Rex Smith was also one of several contributors to the book, with his very fitting foreword. The other contributors, in addition to Darryl McGrath and Howard Healy, are Phillip Blanchard, Bill Federman, Fred LeBrun, Dan Lynch, and Robert Whitcomb. All knew Jim in different ways during his career, and their introductions reflected that fact: No two read alike. Although Jim's writing had a consistently distinctive tone, each contributor saw different qualities in Jim's personality that inspired his writing.

Several people who had known Jim for many years graciously read the manuscript before publication and provided comments about it for use by SUNY Press. They are Michael Larabee of *The Washington Post*; Ben Weller of *Newsday*; Sam Roe of *The Chicago Tribune*, and Jerry Jennings, Mayor of Albany from 1994 to 2013. We greatly appreciate their time and their written comments about the book, each one of which captures a different aspect of Jim's knowledge and skill as an editorial writer.

We decided to reproduce several tributes written after Jim's death, as part of the timeline of his career, and we are grateful for how well they capture Jim's personality and his mentoring qualities. We especially thank Steve Barnes, who wrote the *Times Union*'s news story about his dear friend's death and did what journalists do best, under the most difficult of circumstances: He set aside his personal feelings to produce a vivid portrait of Jim that was published not only in the *Times Union* but by a number of news outlets and journalism websites.

We also would like to acknowledge other tributes, as well as the permission to reproduce them here, by the *Times Union* editorial board; by Lauren Mineau, a former journalism student at the State University of New York, Albany, former editor-in-chief of the *Albany Student Press*, and the last student intern to work with Jim; and by the Newspaper Guild of Albany, of which Jim was an activist past member and a continued supporter, even after he moved into an exempt position in the newsroom.

Kelly Lynch, the daughter of Jim's great friend Dan Lynch, worked swiftly and graciously to grant us permission to use her father's contribution for this book, which Dan completed after he had learned that he had the cancer that would eventually kill him. Dan never saw his work in the finished book, but we think he would have been pleased with the results. He paid tribute to his long friendship with Jim by delivering a eulogy at Jim's memorial service, and he also managed to get a badly needed laugh that day in the church with an insider's joke about a long-ago *Times Union* editor.

John DeRosier very generously gave Jim and me the original of his delightful cartoon about George W. Bush's inauguration, and he inscribed it to Jim after it had been published in the *Times Union*. We could never have imagined the circumstances under which this cartoon would be published a second time. Thanks to John and his wife Tania for their continued friendship.

Two photographs of Jim in his teen years are reproduced in the book, and for those, Darryl wishes to thank Jim's best friend from childhood, Fran "Pancho" Cusack, and his wife, Marie Armstrong. Both of these photographs—the only known copies of them—were part of an album of photographs from Jim's life that Fran and Marie compiled for Jim and Darryl as an engagement gift. Because Jim was orphaned in college and most of his childhood mementoes were discarded when the family home was sold, it's a small miracle that Fran and Marie had these photographs.

Working together as coeditors on this book proved to be a delightful experience. It was far more fun than bittersweet, and we quickly realized that we had an almost seamless shared vision of how we wanted the manuscript to take shape. We had known each other for 20 years when we started this project, and Howard Healy initially worked in an advisory role. It quickly became apparent that his editorial judgment, his priceless institutional memory of the *Times Union*'s editorial board, and his strong grasp of local, state, and national politics and Albany history for the 20 years that this book covers all but demanded that he come on board as a coeditor. The book really took off when he did, because of his long experience as an editor and writer. To that, Darryl added her intimate understanding of how Jim felt about his work, which proved helpful in the selection of the more personal pieces. Darryl possessed the only copies of some of these pieces, and it is fitting that they be preserved in this book and introduced to a wider readership now.

Our thanks to the production staff of the syndicated Canadian Broadcasting Corporation radio news show *As It Happens* for locating the audio clip of an interview with Jim for that show, and for granting permission for us to reproduce the transcript here.

We are extremely grateful to Jeffrey St. Clair, editor of *Counterpunch*, for granting permission for the reproduction of Jim's 2005 *Counterpunch* opinion piece, "Voter Beware."

State University of New York Press was wonderful to work with on this project. Special thanks to James Peltz, codirector of SUNY Press, for immediately recognizing the value of an anthology of Jim's writing, which is in keeping with the mission of this academic press to document the history, culture, and noteworthy people in New York. We would also like to thank Donna Dixon, co-director of SUNY Press, for her support and encouragement. Donna and James work as a seamless partnership, and we are grateful that their combined interest steered this book.

At SUNY Press, we would also like to thank Laurie Searl, for her work as production editor, and also for her beautiful design, which so exactly fit our vision of the book; Dana Foote, for her thoughtful, considerate and expert copy editing; Rafael Chaiken, for being more organized than we were; and Kate Seburyamo and Janice Vunk, for their help with promotions and sales.

Joe Puttrock at McGreevy ProLab in Albany worked his customary magic on some very old photos to make them suitable for reproduction here. He did an especially fine job with a photograph of Jim taken with an inexpensive film camera in 2001 that became the cover shot of the book. Of all the photographs taken of Jim over the years either reading a newspaper or scrutinizing the headlines in the newspaper boxes on a street—and there were many—this one, shot on Duck Harbor Beach in Wellfleet, Cape Cod, Massachusetts, in September 2001, best conveyed the special love Jim had for newspapers. This photograph also captures the complete, utter absorption with which he read a newspaper, all the while automatically critiquing, editing, and rewriting in his head as he turned the pages.

—Darryl McGrath and Howard Healy
Albany, New York
January 2019

Index

Page numbers in italics refer to illustrations or photos, and their captions.

Raines, Howell (former editor at *New York Times*), and John Kennedy O'Hara, 46

Ramos, Benjamin, and illegal voting, 43

Ravena-Coeymans-Selkirk School District, and Jim McGrath's editorials on, 169

Real IRA (breakaway faction of the IRA after 1998 peace accord), 60

Reagan, Ronald, 52, 54–56

Record American (Boston newspaper), 140

Red Sox. *See under* Boston Red Sox

Reno, Janet (former United States Attorney General), and Unabomber case, 85–86

Republican Party 1984 presidential convention and Nancy Pelosi, page 55–56

Ristorante Paradiso, 20

Roberts, Needham (World War I soldier saved by Sergeant Henry Johnson), 15

Robinson, Lamel Wells (Washington Park homicide victim), 7–8

Romano, Jon, 75, 94–95

Rosenfeld, Harry (former editor of the *Times Union*), 167

Rust Belt, 7

Sandburg, Carl, 17, 143

Sandusky, Jerry, and sex abuse scandal at Penn State, 133–134

San Francisco, and Nancy Pelosi as "San Francisco Democrat," 55–56

Saturday Night Live, and John Belushi parody of Thomas P. "Tip" O'Neill Jr., 53

Scaringe, David (civilian shot and killed by Albany police officers), 23–24

Schoharie Valley, 154

Schumer, Charles, Senator, 15, 51, Letter to *Times Union* editorial board about death of Jim McGrath, 79

Selective prosecution. *See under* John Kennedy O'Hara

September 11, 2001, terrorist attacks. *See under* 9/11 terrorist attacks

Sheehan, Kathy (Albany mayor), 29

Shelton, Henry, General (former chairman of the Joint Chiefs of Staff), 15–16

Silver, Sheldon (former New York State Assembly speaker), 42

Sinn Fein Party, 60

Sixth Ward, Albany Common Council, and Paul Webster's candidacy, 20

Skidmore College, and recall of student newspaper, 114

Smith, Marion Roach, and acknowledgement of at Jim McGrath's memorial service, 175

Smith, Patricia
plagiarism accusation and flaws as a *Boston Globe* columnist, 102, 106–107, 109
reading in Albany, 1998, 106

Smith, Rex
acknowledgement of at Jim McGrath's memorial service, 175
on Jim McGrath's death, 170
on Jim McGrath's skill as an editorial writer, xi–xii

Soares, David (Albany County district attorney), 25–26

Spitzer, Bernard (father of Eliot Spitzer), 49

Spitzer, Eliot, 36, 48–50

Spitzer, Silda Wall, and prostitution scandal of Eliot Spitzer, 49

Stanford University, and half-time show mocking Irish famine and genocide, 125–126

State Street (Albany)
food vendors, 13
scene of Albany police shooting of David Scaringe and makeshift shrine in his memory, 23–24

Stentor (student newspaper of Lake Forest College), 174

Stowers, Freddie (Medal of Honor recipient), 15–16

structuring, as a federal financial crime, 49

Sullivan, Joseph (Republican mayoral candidate in Albany, 2001), 19